W9-DFT-059

WITHDRAWN

SHAKESPEARE'S SONNETS

The Problems Solved

A BOOK

SHAKESPEARE'S SONNETS
THE PROBLEMS SOLVED

A Modern Edition,
with Prose Versions, Introduction and Notes

by

A. L. ROWSE

SECOND EDITION

HARPER & ROW, PUBLISHERS
New York, Evanston, San Francisco, London

SHAKESPEARE'S SONNETS: THE PROBLEMS SOLVED. Copyright © 1964, 1973 by A. L. Rowse. All rights reserved. Printed in the United States of America. No part of this book may be used or reproduced in any manner whatsoever without written permission except in the case of brief quotations embodied in critical articles and reviews. For information address Harper & Row, Publishers, Inc., 10 East 53rd Street, New York, N.Y. 10022.

FIRST U.S. EDITION

ISBN: 0-06-013694-4

LIBRARY OF CONGRESS CATALOG CARD NUMBER: 72-10682

CONTENTS

To
Geoffrey Hudson
who has always understood
in lifelong affection

INTRODUCTION TO THE SECOND EDITION

I
This Edition

Hitherto the Sonnets of Shakespeare have been regarded as the greatest puzzle in English, possibly world, literature. Their problems have been thought to be insoluble, the questions they raise unanswerable. In default of answers, certain and valid, — these poems — among the world's most famous and beautiful — have long provided ground for the wildest speculation. Even among scholars there has been no certainty, but utter confusion. Their very nature has been in dispute, some respectable scholars thinking them to have been mere literary exercises.

They were, of course, autobiographical ; they would not have the power, the urgency and conviction they carry, if they had not been. They were autobiography before they became literature. They come straight from the heart, from the whole personality — as great literature does — of the world's best loved writer. Naturally, with a professional writer, they have here and there touches of literary exercise ; but, as a whole, they tell a story so strange that it could only have been experienced and true.

It is the purpose of this edition to bring out the story, as none has been able to do, and to show that it *is* true. One cannot fully appreciate the Sonnets without reading them as a whole : no use reaching one down here or there and then hoping to grasp the situation and what one is being told. Yet that is what people usually do.

The Sonnets were never written to create a puzzle — though the clue has been lost for centuries. They were written straightforwardly, directly, by one person for another — by a poet for his young patron, as we shall see — with an immediate and sincere impulse. Yet the story that is revealed, and has been concealed for so long, is highly dramatic and that of a poet who was already beginning to be well known as a dramatist. That is why they were not published at the time, like other sonnet-sequences ; they were not published till years after the story they relate was folded up, and then not by Shakespeare, but by a publisher who had *got* the manuscripts. They were too near the bone.

This is where an historian is needed — though an historian with an equal feeling for literature. The textual scholar, Hyder Rollins, who gave us the fullest edition of the Sonnets in the *New Variorum Shakespeare*, saw that the indispensable clue to their interpretation was to get their dating right. 'The question when the Sonnets were written is in many respects the most important of all the unanswerable questions they pose. If it could be answered definitely and finally, there might be some chance of establishing to general satisfaction the identity of the friend, the rival poet (supposing that all were real individuals), and even of determining whether the order of the Quarto is the author's or not. In the past and at present such a solution has been and remains an idle dream.'

Observe the total pessimism, the assumption that all these questions are unanswerable. 'The problems of Shakespeare's Sonnets are insoluble ; *therefore* they are insoluble' — that was the obtuse attitude I came up against in putting forward the correct answers, both in my biographies of Shakespeare, Marlowe and Southampton, as well as in my previous edition of the Sonnets. I never expected to find the answer to the most mysterious, the most tantalising and elusive problem of them all — the identity of Shakespeare's mistress, the Dark Lady.

Of course one would never find her by the reach-me-down method of throwing a name up in the air, hoping that it would settle in a preconceived slot — any more than one could settle the identity of 'Mr. W. H.' that way. That way is no method at all ; all the books written that way have naturally not solved the problem but merely added to the confusion, a waste of time, so many mares' nests.

As I have said all along, the proper method is an historical one : to take each poem one after the other, to follow it line by line, watching for every piece of internal information for its coherence with what is happening in the external world, checking for consistency at every point, accumulating patiently every fact and what may legitimately be inferred, until the whole structure stands forth clear. I said originally that it would be found that the historian's account of the matter could not be impugned.

Nor has it been. In fact, it has been triumphantly vindicated by the wholly unexpected discovery of the Dark Lady and who she was, along these lines in complete consistency with my previous findings.

All the questions are now answered 'definitely and finally', as Hyder Rollins and so many others have wished for so long. This definiteness and finality could never be achieved by the road of literary conjecture ; only by precise dating and by following simple and rigorous historical method. In the sterilising specialisation of this age it seems to have been regarded with some recalcitrance by literary folk that an historian should assail these problems, and with anything but a generous response that he should solve these for them. But Elizabethans were not given to abortive specialisation : that was contrary to the whole spirit of the Renaissance, when a Ralegh could be both soldier and sailor, courtier and poet, historian and chemist ; a Bacon, lawyer, philosopher and scientist. Shakespeare was completely a man of the theatre ; even so, he was actor, playwright, poet, producer, part-owner and could turn his hand to anything, a perfect 'Johannes Factotum' as his envious rival, Robert Greene, described him.

It is a reflection on this age to have to remind them that, immersed as this historian has long been in the study of the Elizabethans, he shares their attitude on this, and even their practice, himself a poet.

A word, then, about this edition and the method it follows.

It is intended to be practical and common sense, with the whole emphasis on making the Sonnets intelligible to the modern reader. There is no point in sticking to archaic spelling or Elizabethan punctuation. Shakespeare had no use for pedantry and laughed at pedants. In any case there were misprints in the original edition ; it is generally accepted from this that Shakespeare had not read the proofs — as he had those of *Venus and Adonis* and *Lucrece*.

Actually my text is closer to the original and more conservative than any other. The historian who has been habituated to Elizabethan usage all his life and has read thousands of original documents, finds their language becomes second nature to him. This has useful literary consequences. Many people misjudge the relations between the poet and his patron by thinking of the high-flown language in modern terms : they are not sufficiently deep in the age to know that this was the proper decorum for a gentlemanly poet to use to a handsome young nobleman. Even textually, an Elizabethan scholar realises that there is no need for the emendations and interferences with the text that Georgian and Victorian editors felt called upon to make. They are just not necessary.

So I give the best text of each sonnet that I can arrive at, in modern spelling and punctuation — they are not always easily intelligible otherwise. On one page I give the sonnet, opposite it a prose version, and below that the commentary on it.

The object of the version in modern prose is again *intelligibility*, to bring out the meaning. Here, too, I have been conservative rather than adventurous : I have kept closely to Shakespeare's own words, so far as the differing rhythms of prose and verse allow. Translating Elizabethan verse into the prose of today brings great rewards. I know that this is true, for other people as for myself, that we have been reading the Sonnets all our lives often without knowing precisely what they were saying, without being sure of the meaning and sense of some passages and lines. Now we shall have not only the background, the persons and their circumstances, the changing situation with regard to each other, but the meaning and sense of the text.

Sometimes the commentary occupies only a few lines ; occasionally it is much more lengthy and runs over the page, when the topical and other content requires explanation and yields us valuable information. My aim has been to reduce commentary to only what is necessary. There is no point in cluttering up the page with nonsensical suggestions only to refute them, or with a pretentious apparatus of criticism which often reveals that the editor has not understood the sense. One should not mix up the scaffolding with the building ; when the building is up and stands on its own the scaffolding comes down.

The aim is to let what Shakespeare says stand forth clear, and simply to clarify what may be obscure or to bring out what lurks behind the text. Particularly in regard to contemporary events and happenings, for those confirm the dating for us and that, as Hyder Rollins saw, provides the clue to everything else. (Correct dating requires an historian ; literary conjectures have been all over the place with their dates, often show no conception of the decisive and determining importance of a date : hence much of the confusion.) But verbal parallels with Shakespeare's poems and plays not only corroborate the dating but confirm his experiences, thoughts and feelings at the time. Lastly, I have given the meaning of rare or difficult words and phrases — those that need explaining, not those that do not.

There really is no need for anything more. With this done for the reader, he should be able now to read the Sonnets for the story they unfold as well as for the poetry — I originally said, like a novel, but perhaps for the *drama* they reveal : an additional play from the hand of Shakespeare, the drama of his own personal life in the decisive years of his career.

II
The Publisher's Mr. W. H.

The first thing to realise is that the Sonnets were not published until many years after the experiences they relate were over. That is very understandable when we come to consider the nature of the experiences, whom they affected and how near the bone they were. They were not published until 1609, only seven years before Shakespeare's death ; the experiences they describe go back to the years 1592 to 1594-5, a decade or more before.

We need not go into details about publication, printing, typography : we need only to say that the people involved — publisher, printer, booksellers — were all reputable people. The publisher, Thomas Thorpe, was rather remarkable among publishers. He was himself literary-minded, he had a notably distinguished list, published a number of famous plays, particularly Ben Jonson's and Chapman's, as well as Marlowe's translation of Lucan ; and Thorpe was a friend of Edward Blount, Marlowe's friend.

We do not know whether Shakespeare had anything to do with the publication. Thorpe had got the manuscripts from 'Mr. W. H.' — this was regular enough in Elizabethan publishing — and it was Thorpe who wrote the somewhat flowery dedication to 'Mr. W. H.', full of gratitude for having got the manuscript of the Sonnets for him, as well he might be. A study of Thorpe shows that eloquent dedications were characteristic of him. But the essential point to remember is that 'Mr. W. H.' — we shall come to him later — was not Shakespeare's man at all, but Thorpe's, the publisher's.

Scores, if not hundreds, of books and articles have been written under the misapprehension that 'Mr. W. H.' was the young lord to whom Shakespeare wrote the Sonnets. All these books are beside the mark. We need not consider any of them, merely point out that such eminent Shakespeare scholars as Sir Edmund Chambers and Professor Dover Wilson, let alone others, incomprehensibly overlooked this elementary fact and ruined their work in this regard by trying to find a 'Mr. W. H.' who fitted the character of Shakespeare's young 'Lord of my love'.

Let us repeat : 'Mr. W. H.' was simply Thorpe's dedicatee. We shall note later who he was — a mattter of secondary importance — in its proper place at the end of the story. But the realisation of this obvious fact is the indispensable condition to getting the Sonnets right : it opens the way to common sense about them and their correct interpretation.

III

Shakespeare's Patron : Southampton

The Sonnets were written to and for the obvious person, Shakespeare's patron, the young Earl of Southampton, like the two long poems publicly dedicated to him in these same years. These were *Venus and Adonis* in 1593, written therefore 1592–3, and *Lucrece* in 1594, written therefore 1593–4. People unaware of conditions at the time naturally do not know how critical these years were for Shakespeare — though he tells us so plainly enough in the Sonnets. Both 1592 and 1593 were years of severe plague : the theatres were mostly closed, conditions were bad for touring the country, we know that one company came back broken, that the family of one well-known actor (Robert Browne) was wiped out. This is one reason why the circumstances of the companies were so confused at this period, their affairs impossible to sort out. As to some of the dire consequences of these critical years we should have the imagination to note that in 1592 there died Robert Greene and Thomas Watson, Marlowe's friend, poet and connoisseur of music ; in 1593 Marlowe was killed ; in the winter of 1593–4 Thomas Kyd died, a leading tragedian with his *Spanish Tragedy* ; and in the next twelve-month George Peele disappeared.

When the cloud lifted in 1594 and the Lord Chamberlain's Company was founded, Shakespeare had things very much his own way until the rise of Ben Jonson a few years later. But meanwhile what was he to do, with the theatres closed and a wife and three children to support at Stratford ?

He was saved and provided for by the patronage of Southampton. No wonder he was so deeply grateful and expresses his love and devotion to the young peer : he says that his

> . . . life no longer than thy love will stay,
> For it depends upon that love of thine.

The great majority of literary scholars, since Malone in the eighteenth century, have seen that the young man of the Sonnets was Southampton — this is in fact the traditional view — and that they cohere entirely in theme and language with *Venus and Adonis* and *Lucrece*.

And when, indeed, would Shakespeare be writing his Sonnets, except in these years, when time allowed and circumstances compelled ? But Southampton and his family provided other opportunities for him as both dramatist and actor during these years when he might otherwise have been idle and in want. We now know that *Love's Labour's Lost* was written as a private skit on and for the Southampton circle by its poet, in 1593 ; and that *A Midsummer Night's Dream* was adapted for performance to mark the private nuptials of the elderly couple, Southampton's mother and Sir Thomas Heneage, Vice-Chamberlain of the Queen's Household, which took place on 2 May 1594. *Romeo and Juliet* reflects, if no more, the poet's interest in the Danvers–Long feud, which culminated in the killing of Henry Long by Henry Danvers, Southampton's dearest friend. (John Florio appeared on the stage in that affair — as no doubt he appeared on the private stage of *Love's Labour's Lost*.)[1]

Shakespeare's language to his patron in dedicating his poems, and the attitude it expresses, have often been commented upon. We need only note here that in offering *Venus and Adonis* in 1593 he promises 'to take advantage of all idle hours till I have honoured you with some graver labour'. If it fails, he would 'never after ear [*i.e.* plough] so barren a land. . . . Your Honour's in all duty, William Shakespeare.'

Notice the phrase 'in all duty' : this is regular Elizabethan usage and means that Shakespeare is the Earl's poet. Notice also that at the very beginning of the Sonnets, Sonnet 3, there is the same curious contryman's word 'ear' meaning to plough, in the phrase 'uneared womb'. In Sonnet 26, the *Envoi* which concludes the first section, the theme of duty is thrice asserted :

> Lord of my love, to whom in vassalage
> Thy merit hath my duty strongly knit,
> To thee I send my written ambassage
> To witness duty, not to show my wit.
> Duty so great . . .

Those whose ear is attuned to Elizabethan usage will recognise at once the double sense in which '*Lord* of my love' is used, both general and literal : the Sonnets were written to a lord, and that lord was the patron.

[1] For fuller detail, cf. my *William Shakespeare: A Biography*, chaps. x and xi.

Persons of any sensibility have also noticed the increase of warmth and affection between the dedication of *Venus and Adonis* in 1593 and that of *Lucrece* in 1594. The latter begins, 'the love I dedicate to your lordship is without end' : even allowing for the high-flown language of the Elizabethans — 'love' where we should say 'devotion' — I do not know of any Elizabethan dedication which strikes quite such a note. 'What I have done is yours, what I have to do is yours, being part of all I have, devoted yours.' We shall see, when we come to consider the young Lord's relations with Shakespeare's mistress, the Dark Lady, how the phrase 'being part of all I have' echoes his sentiment expressed in the Sonnets :

> Take all my loves, my love, yea, take them all . . .
> I cannot blame thee for my love thou usest . . .
> I do forgive thy robbery, gentle thief,
> Although thou steal thee all my poverty.

Again, in the dedication, Shakespeare subscribes himself twice over in all duty ; for all his independence of spirit and insistence on being taken for a gentleman, he was in these years partly dependent on his patron.

And yet the year 1593 witnesses a remarkable growth of warmth in their relations, an emotional involvement which concerns not only Shakespeare's now complex feelings for his young lord — gratitude, affection, a recognition of his golden nature, a certain protectiveness towards a fatherless youth exposed to all the temptations of his position, concern, alarm, reproach — but also Shakespeare's apprehension from a rival poet he recognises to be his superior, his infatuation for the Dark Lady, the repercussions of both these upon his relationship with his young patron. The fundamental complication is that of his feelings for Southampton. It is all very complex : no wonder so many Victorian, and Victorian-minded, commentators have been baffled by it. One simply cannot get it right, or begin to understand it, in terms of middle-class Victorian morality, with all its inhibitions and imperceptions. One must see it in terms of a Renaissance Court-life, of Elizabethan high society. Fortunately today's more open, permissive society is in a position to understand and express what has given earlier academics so much embarrassment.

For the present it is sufficient to note that it is in 1593 that the complication of the plot begins.

We need not go in much detail here into the close parallels in theme and language between the early sonnets with *Venus and Adonis*, and those of the later with *Lucrece*. They are indeed obvious, and we shall point them out in the commentary. The situation of Southampton in these years is quite well known : it is precisely and in every respect that of the young lord of the Sonnets. It appears again as the theme of *Venus and Adonis* and of *Love's Labour's Lost* — that of the handsome and attractive young man who will not, as yet, respond to women. (This is very unlike William Shakespeare, who was all too responsive, a highly sexed heterosexual from every evidence.)

In 1592, when the Sonnets begin, the young Earl came of age at eighteen ; born on 6 October 1573, it was time for the head of a noble house to marry, all the more so because he was its last male representative. His father had died in 1581, leaving his boy to succeed to the peerage at the age of eight. It was still more urgent because the family, though ennobled by Henry VIII, had remained Catholic and needed protection. The great Lord Burghley, the Queen's Lord Treasurer, had a protective attitude towards the peerage and an eye to the main chance for his own family, the Cecils. The Lord Treasurer had had the boy under his supervision and had a suitable wife waiting for him in his granddaughter, Lady Elizabeth Vere, daughter of the irresponsible Oxford, who had ruined himself and his estates. The girl needed to be provided for and would be ; Burghley had got some kind of assurance out of the boy that he would marry her when he came of age.

But when he came of age he would not go through with it. Every kind of pressure was applied to him. His mother begged for a postponement : 'I do not find a disposition in my son to be tied as yet ; what will be hereafter time will try, and no want shall be found on my behalf.' Lord Burghley applied to the youth's grandfather, Lord Montagu — who got from the young man 'this general answer that your Lordship was this last winter well pleased to yield unto him a further respite of one year'. The year was almost up, but still the young man would not marry and do his duty by his family.

The fact was that he was not as yet interested in women ; we know independently that he was ambivalent, rather feminine in appearance with his long golden tresses over the left shoulder. He had an emotional attachment — there is no evidence that it was a sexual one — to Essex, the *preux chevalier* of his order, successor to Sir Philip Sidney as the darling of the younger generation. Southampton would have followed him anywhere, and did, so far as he was allowed — to fight under him in Normandy in 1591 when he was only seventeen, then on the Azores Expedition in 1597, in Ireland in 1599, and almost to die with Essex on the scaffold in 1601. He was loyal and generous to a fault ; he had a golden nature, everybody recognised, and was popular and beloved all his life. But he was rash and remained for too long an adolescent ; like so many young Elizabethan aristocrats he was self-willed and spoilt. One sees the dangers life would hold for him.

He might have been steadied by an earlier marriage. Shakespeare was persuaded to join in the campaign to urge him to marry — and this would have been very agreeable to his mother, the Countess. Shakespeare would have met him a little before the Sonnets began — there were plenty of other writers out for his patronage, Nashe among them, books dedicated to him. Florio was his Italian tutor and dedicated his *World of Words* to him in the obsequious terms of a household servant, which he was. Not so Shakespeare, who, though he becomes his poet and has the proper deference to a peer, always writes as an independent gentleman. The relationship and its consequences for literature — not only the Sonnets, the poems written for Southampton, but the plays connected with the household, *Love's Labour's Lost, A Midsummer Night's Dream* and, to some extent, *Romeo and Juliet* — produced something unique.

The Sonnets take their rise then in Southampton's known situation, the duty lying upon him to marry, beget an heir, and carry on his house. Naturally, in such a situation, an Elizabethan poet begins courteously, eloquently, in praise of the youth's beauty, reflecting his mother's :

> Thou art thy mother's glass, and she in thee
> Calls back the lovely April of her prime.

He should beget an heir to carry on his looks :

> Now is the time that face should form another.

All the more so because he is fatherless, the last of his house :

> dear my love, you know
> You had a father : let your son say so.

Not to do so would be neglecting his plain duty,

> Seeking that beauteous roof to ruinate
> Which to repair should be thy chief desire.

But the young man would not and did not marry for some years ; until in 1598 Elizabeth Vernon, one of the Queen's ladies caught him by getting pregnant, and Essex, who was her cousin, made him reluctantly marry her. That was some years ahead, when all the experiences related in the Sonnets had been over for more than three years.

The Dating and Order of the Sonnets

There really is no difficulty in dating the Sonnets, for an Elizabethan historian who can read the topical references to events at the time : they yield a consistent and firm scheme in time, and they are in an intelligible order as they are.

The first section of the Sonnets ends with an *Envoi*, Sonnet 26, 'Lord of my love', a suitable 'ambassage' to the patron. In Sonnet 25 we are given our first signpost :

> Great princes' favourites their fair leaves spread
> But as the marigold at the sun's eye,
> And in themselves their pride lies burièd,
> For, at a frown, they in their glory die.
> The painful warrior famousèd for fight,
> After a thousand victories once foiled,
> Is from the book of honour razèd quite
> And all the rest forgot for which he toiled.

This is an obvious description of the fall of the favourite, Sir Walter Ralegh, in the summer of 1592. There is his personality quite recognisable : 'painful' in Elizabethan English means 'painstaking'. The famous warrior was regarded at the time as no less hard-working ; in this very year Sir Robert Cecil wrote of him, 'he can toil terribly'. Ralegh himself wrote of his fall, having been caught in the usual way by Elizabeth Throckmorton, one of the Queen's young ladies, 'once amiss, all is lost'. Compare 'once foiled'. No doubt these phrases echoed at Court.

Sonnet 86 yields us our next signpost. For a brief period, from Sonnet 79 to 85, Shakespeare is much concerned with the rivalry of another poet, whom he recognises as a superior. (What is he rivalling Shakespeare for, but the patronage of the patron ? — *i.e.* the Sonnets are written for the patron. Q.E.D.) We shall analyse the sonnets in place — the references to 'the worthier pen', 'that able spirit', his lettered sophistication, his 'polished' and 'well-refinèd' pen — and the clear parallels between *Venus and Adonis* and

xix

Hero and Leander, which Shakespeare and Marlowe were writing in rivalry for Southampton. Marlowe's poem was only half-finished when he was killed on 30 May 1593, and it was not published till 1598. But the verbal echoes show that each knew the other's poem in manuscript.

The point here, however, is that all these sonnets dealing with the Rival Poet are in the present tense, the rivalry is briefly in being — until it comes to a sudden end with Sonnet 86, all in the past tense. Something has happened to the Rival : he has disappeared ; he is not mentioned again : the whole tone of the sonnet is valedictory :

> Was it the proud full sail of his great verse ? . . .

Everyone at the time would recognise to whom that referred : Marlowe's achievement had been to marry 'great verse' to the drama ; no previous dramatist had been a great poet : he was. Shakespeare recognises his superiority, up to the hour of his death ; Ben Jonson, in his tribute to Shakespeare in the First Folio sums up his earlier rival's characteristic achievement in the phrase, 'Marlowe's mighty line'.

Marlowe is now dead. We need go no further here : with Sonnet 86 we are in the early summer of 1593.

Our next signpost has given rise to more confusion than any : Sonnet 107, with its reference to 'the mortal moon'. Yet, to anyone with any sense of logic along with historical sense, it gives us mathematical certainty. For it contains *two* topical references, and these two events *must* be taking place at one and the same time,

> The mortal moon hath her eclipse endured . . .

In Elizabethan parlance 'the mortal moon' always refers to the Queen — sometimes terrene or terrestrial moon, or Cynthia, goddess of the moon ; but always the moon, virginal and chaste. What this line means is that she has emerged from an eclipse, *i.e.* a shadow upon her.

But this must be at the same time as the event referred to in the same quatrain :

> Incertainties now crown themselves assured,
> And peace proclaims olives of endless age.

The peace that ended people's uncertainties and gave promise of extending itself, as indeed it did, was the peace brought about by the submission of Paris to Henri IV (in March 1594, which ended the ferocious civil wars that had racked France ever since 1564 — all through Shakespeare's life so far). It led shortly to peace between France and Spain, and gave promise of a general settlement in western Europe.

At the very same time the Queen had emerged from the shadow upon her life, of the supposed conspiracy of her personal physician, Dr. Lopez, to poison her. This unfortunate Jew had earned the hatred of Essex for divulging that he was suffering from a sexual complaint ; at the same time his success as a doctor went to his head, and he dabbled in political intelligence with Spain. Spanish agents offered him a large bribe to kill Elizabeth, though she never believed that he closed with them or had any intention of harming her. Essex engaged his 'honour' in pursuing him to the death, and Lopez could not clear himself. He was hustled off to the Tower, and on 28 February was tried at the Guildhall by a commission over which Essex presided. In Elizabethan England, as in totalitarian countries in our time, if a man could not establish his innocence then he was guilty.

He was sentenced to death. But the Queen would not sign his death-warrant. For more than three months she held out against her favourite and public opinion. For the affair led to a disgraceful outburst of anti-Jewish sentiment ; it gave occasion for the revival of Marlowe's play *The Jew of Malta*, which inspired Shakespeare in the next year to write *The Merchant of Venice*. The Lopez case made a sensation ; of course popular opinion was always with Essex and thought that the Queen had been exposed to grave danger. At length she was forced to give way to pressure, and on 7 June Lopez was hanged.

These two events took place at the same time in the spring of 1594 : their convergence makes it certain that that is the period we reach with Sonnet 107.

With the penultimate sonnet in the Southampton sequence, Sonnet 124, we reach the winter of that year, 1594-5.

The very first line,

> If my dear love were but the child of state,

confirms that the subject of these sonnets is a person of state — as he was : a peer of the realm. This is again corroborated in the last sonnet devoted solely to him, Sonnet 125 :

> Were't aught to me I bore the canopy,

i.e. a canopy of state over him, an appropriate image. Sonnet 124 is full of the politico-religious issue of the time, the government's campaign against the infiltrating Jesuits and seminary priests. Though Southampton's mother and father were Catholics, there is no evidence that Southampton was a practising — and he certainly was not a political — Catholic, unlike his father.

The government point of view was that the Jesuits were a Fifth Column operating in time of war. This winter saw a severe campaign against the Jesuits and seminary priests ; more of them were executed than at any time since Armada year. Shakespeare, as usual, expresses the ordinary patriotic view with regard to these people, who regarded themselves as martyrs for their religion. He describes them as

> the fools of time,
> Which die for goodness who have lived for crime,

This, however, is not the point with which we are concerned ; the point is that the Southampton sequence ends here, in the winter of 1594-5. The topical references confirm theme, language, parallels : everything holds together and shows that these experiences occupied the three years from 1592. Towards the end of the Southampton sequence, in Sonnet 104, Shakespeare himself corroborates this :

> Three winters cold
> Have from the forests shook three summers' pride,
> Three beauteous springs to yellow autumn turned
> In process of the seasons have I seen,
> Three April perfumes in three hot Junes burned,
> Since first I saw you fresh, which yet are green.

The three years which the Sonnets cover up to Sonnet 104 ran from the winter of 1591-2 to 1594. The next sonnet, 105, assured Southampton that

> . . . all alike my songs and praises be
> To one, of one, still such, and ever so.

The 'songs and praises' would include the poems and dedications to him : there was no other patron.

The next sonnet, 126, is just a buffer about Cupid, to mark the division, for immediately after come the sonnets which record Shakespeare's tormented affair with his mistress, the Dark Lady. They go right on to the end in numbering, with a return to a fanciful playing with Cupid in relation to the affair — the poet 'distempered' needing 'the help of bath' (probably the help of the baths at Bath, regular Elizabethan treatment for this distemper) — in the last couple of sonnets. But they serve to wind the affair up, briefly and salutarily.

Nor is there any reason to think that the Dark Lady sonnets are out of order ; they have an order of their own, and their own development : from the charm of the first approach to rapid disillusionment ; but there is the infatuation, the spell he cannot get away from, alarm and torment for the golden youth he has involved with her. In these Sonnets 127-154, later in numbering, Shakespeare is writing primarily of the affair from his point of view. In Sonnets 34-42 he has already touched on it in its earlier stages as it affected his young patron. And that relates to the year 1593.

Thus Sonnets 127-154, though later in numbering, are not later in time ; they come within the Southampton sequence, and all relate to the years 1593-4, the years of *Love's Labour's Lost* with its dark lady, Rosaline, and *Lucrece* with its guilt-laden atmosphere and remorse of conscience.

Everything consistently holds together : there would be no point in trying to insert the Dark Lady Sonnets into the Southampton sequence, for they have a different angle — Shakespeare's involvement with her rather than Southampton's and its effect on the relations between poet and patron.

It is significant that the Rival Poet has nothing whatever to do with this : that episode was brief ; in any case the Dark Lady would have no charms for Marlowe, for he was entirely homosexual.

There are no more topical references in the Sonnets ; those we have are sufficient — enough to give us not only firm and consistent dating, but certainty. It remains only to say that this is in keeping with the conservative, traditional view ; earlier literary scholars usually felt that Shakespeare's Sonnets belonged to the first half of the 1590s, when the sonneteering vogue was at its height. The historian has been able to make this quite certain — no longer a matter of conjecture — from the topical references to events at the time. This makes an indispensable junction of the internal world of the Sonnets with the external world of history, the corroboration of their subjective world with objective events. This is the only method by which the questions could be answered, the problems solved.

Thus the Sonnets offer an integrated, artistic whole. There is no point in rearranging or disarranging or deranging them, though many such efforts have been made. Still less did Shakespeare write sonnets all over the place — at any time from the Spanish Armada to the death of the Queen or beyond, right up to date of publication. People who put forward that idea evidently have no idea of dating or its determining importance. Hyder Rollins had : he saw quite rightly that it held the clue, and only along this path would the answers be found.

V
The Story: its Outlines

We do not need to recount the story that the Sonnets describe — better to leave it to them and the commentary — but simply to bring forward the main points that stand out, explain what requires elucidation and what was so important for Shakespeare and his work in the relationship. It began in Shakespeare's urging the young man to marry, but it soon developed into the poet's responding to the charm of the young aristocrat into whose intimacy he was privileged to enter. Renaissance people had a highly idealised cult of youth, understandable when it was so much more brief and difficult to hold at bay the onset of age in teeth, hair, etc. Shakespeare owed inspiration as well as support to his young patron — and many poets have been in love with the idea of being in love.

It was not at all, on Shakespeare's part, homosexual ; even if we did not know that everything shows that he was extremely heterosexual, with an exceptional fixation on women and their parts, he tells us so in so many words. He describes the rather feminine beauty of the young man — the Renaissance had no Victorian prejudices about this :

> A woman's face with Nature's own hand painted
> Hast thou, the master-mistress of my passion . . .
> A man in hue, all hues in his controlling,
> Which steals men's eyes and women's souls amazeth.

Shakespeare would have been happy to consummate the relationship, if only the youth had been a girl :

> And for a woman wert thou first created,
> Till Nature, as she wrought thee, fell a-doting
> And, by addition, me of thee defeated
> By adding one thing to my purpose nothing.

What could be clearer ? As a man the youth possesses something Shakespeare has no use for. And in case anyone doesn't know what he means, he makes it doubly clear :

But since she pricked thee out for women's pleasure,
Mine be thy love, and thy love's use their treasure.

An amusing way of putting it : the women can have him sexually,
so long as Shakespeare has his love.

I do not think it would be going beyond legitimate bounds to
say here that, the youth being rather feminine and ambivalent, the
poet's masculinity may well have had an added attraction for him.
We need go no further than to point out that the boot is quite on the
other leg from what a number of persons have thought, who were
either imperceptive or had an interested prejudice in the matter :
it was not Shakespeare who was homosexual but the young peer
who would not have minded. This is indisputable ; the rest we may
properly leave to conjecture.

The relationship began, as such experiences do, with the bliss of
mutual discovery ; the difference of age added a further dimension
to it. Shakespeare was nine and a half years older, no longer young
as Elizabethan lives went — and indeed his own life was more than
half over. For him it was the entry into Paradise ; it introduced a
personality particularly qualified to respond into a sophisticated and
cultivated society it must have longed for and from which it had so
much to learn. Studies of Shakespeare's imagery have noticed the
increased refinement of the senses, of taste and smell, of ear and eye,
from this time on. Literary scholars have commented on the world
of difference between the earlier comedies, *The Comedy of Errors*
and *The Two Gentlemen of Verona*, and the inspired works that follow,
A Midsummer Night's Dream and *Romeo and Juliet*. In addition to
support, besides opening closed doors to him, giving him the chance
of his life and at a time of necessity, Shakespeare owed — what is
most important of all to a poet — inspiration to the experience. It
was the turning-point in his life and career.

No wonder gratitude and professed devotion grew into love.
We watch the process in the Sonnets. Then, in 1593, the relationship is harmed and tarnished by Shakespeare's mistress getting hold
of the youth ; Shakespeare is the more disturbed because he recognises that he himself is responsible. He had got his young patron, as
his superior — in regular Elizabethan fashion — to write to the lady
on his behalf :

He learned but surety-like to write for me
Under that bond that him as fast doth bind.

The lady, being what she was, saw a better chance with the young peer, and this was fairly certainly his first experience with women. This redoubled Shakespeare's anxiety. There is not only his loss of his mistress :

> That thou hast her, it is not all my grief,
> And yet it may be said I loved her dearly . . .

More important is the fear of losing Southampton and his friendship :

> That she hath thee is of my wailing chief,
> A loss in love that touches me more nearly.

It is a curious situation psychologically, for Southampton was led on to her by the fact that she was Shakespeare's mistress :

> Thou dost love her because thou know'st I love her.

This is the more understandable, now that we know what Southampton's nature was. It was a distracting situation for the older man, even in its early stage :

> Both find each other, and I lose both twain,
> And both for my sake lay on me this cross.

Shakespeare's good name was already besmirched by it, but he was more anxious that his young patron should not suffer in repute :

> I may not evermore acknowledge thee,
> Lest my bewailèd guilt should do thee shame,
> Nor thou with public kindness honour me,
> Unless thou take that honour from thy name.

We can only conclude that, for relations with her to have this effect, she must have been well known, though not respected, no mere anonymity.

In this situation Shakespeare reproaches the young man not only on his older friend's account,

> Ay me ! but yet thou mightst my seat forbear,

but also on his own, pursuing a forbidden pleasure when he refused to marry,

> By wilful taste of what thyself refusest.

The snake of sex has entered Paradise, innocence been lost, the bliss of their earlier relations tarnished. One thing to bring out here : the indication is that Southampton's affair with Shakespeare's mistress was a briefer episode and altogether less significant and harrowing to the younger man than it was to the older. And that is convincing psychologically : Shakespeare's nature was deeper and capable of greater suffering. But the whole complex of relations has deepened, and with it the power and force of the poems. The friendship between older and younger man can never be quite the same : its pristine purity has gone, apprehension and mistrust have entered in, and with them, grief and anguish, reproaches and self-reproach, the consciousness of guilt, the guilt that lies upon all three.

On the other hand, all this makes for maturing of experience, which is expressed in more powerful, if more sombre, poetry. The complication of the plot is contemporaneous with the guilt-laden atmosphere of *Lucrece* ; all is grist that comes to the poet's, still more the dramatist's, mill. As Rilke answered his young friend, who asked him what makes a poet : 'Mann muss viele erlebnisse ertragen.' (One has to go through a great deal.)

VI
Who was the Dark Lady?

And so we come to the last and most recalcitrant problem of all — the identity of Shakespeare's mistress, the Dark Lady. No one has ever found her, though many have searched. The irony is that one could never find her by looking for her ; I was not looking for her when I stumbled upon her, waiting for me, as she had been waiting in those documents for someone who could identify her, call her back to life after nearly four centuries, give her once more a local habitation and a name.

As I have pointed out, Shakespeare did not write the Sonnets to create a puzzle — they were once all too clear : that is why they were not published until some years had elapsed. The personality of his mistress, as he describes her, is most striking and individual : no one like her in the whole range of sonnet-literature. She was very recognisable.

What does he tell us about her ?

The first thing is that she is extremely dark : black hair, black eyes, brows and eyelashes. This was unfashionable in an age that idealised fair colouring, skin and hair, when fashion was dictated by the Queen with her pale complexion and red-gold hair (later a wig). This made some people regard Shakespeare's mistress — so she was a known figure — as not beautiful :

> some say that thee behold
> Thy face hath not the power to make love groan.

xxvii

She makes Shakespeare groan all right, 'a thousand groans but thinking on thy face', and

> to my dear doting heart
> Thou art the fairest and most precious jewel.

Both in Sonnet 127, the first in the second sequence — devoted to his relations with her — and contemporaneously in *Love's Labour's Lost*, he sings the praises of black colouring and of his Dark Lady. In the play he uses virtually the same words as in the Sonnet :

> No face is fair that is not full so black . . .
> O, if in black my lady's brows be decked,
> It mourns that painting and usurping hair
> Should ravish doters with a false aspect ;
> And therefore is she born to make black fair.

From this we may deduce, as I have pointed out before, that she was a lady who would be known in the Southampton circle. (And also that, when she turns round, as Rosaline in the play, and describes Berowne with his complete devotion to women, it is Shakespeare describing and laughing at himself.)

The second thing that he tells us is that she is musical :

> How oft when thou, my music, music play'st
> Upon that blessèd wood whose motion sounds
> With thy sweet fingers, when thou gently sway'st
> The wiry concord that mine ear confounds,
> Do I envy those jacks [keys] that nimble leap
> To kiss the tender inward of thy hand . . .

The susceptible poet describes himself standing there as she performs upon the virginals, her hands upon the keys,

> O'er whom thy fingers walk with gentle gait
> Making dead wood more blest than living lips.

We soon learn that the Dark Lady is a very equivocal lady ; she is, in fact, a bad lot, as Shakespeare knows very well :

> those lips of thine
> That have profaned their scarlet ornaments
> And sealed false bonds of love as oft as mine,
> Robbed others' beds' revenues of their rents.

He accepts the fact that he is not alone in enjoying her favours, even if his eyes

> Be anchored in the bay where all men ride . . .
> Why should my heart think that a several plot
> Which my heart knows the wide world's common place ?

The answer is that he cannot get away from her spell :

> Whence hast thou this becoming of things ill
> That, in the very refuse of thy deeds,
> There is such strength and warrantise of skill
> That, in my mind, thy worst all best exceeds ?

His eyes are blinded by passion, or perhaps something more, perhaps a spell :

> O, from what power hast thou this powerful might . . .
> To make me give the lie to my true sight ? . . .
> Who taught thee how to make me love thee more,
> The more I hear and see just cause of hate ?

Other people know very well what — and who — she is :

> O, though I love what others do abhor,
> With others thou shouldst not abhor my state.

She dazzles his eyes,

> Which have no correspondence with true sight ;

though others see well enough :

> If that be fair whereon my false eyes dote,
> What means the world to say it is not so ?

The world was right about her : Shakespeare knew that she was false :

> When my love swears that she is made of truth
> I do believe her, though I know she lies.

He accepts the pretence as 'if he were some untutored youth',

> Unlearnèd in the world's false subtleties :

it suits him, for he knows that he is no longer young and she knows that his days are past the best. From this one might infer that she was the younger, but it would only be an inference ; we shall learn that in fact this was the case.

So there was nothing whatever romantic about the relation, as there had been in his idealised friendship with his young patron, before she came into it :

> O, love's best habit is in seeming trust,
> And age in love loves not to have years told.
> Therefore I lie with her and she with me,
> And in our faults by lies we flattered be.

We are told that besides being false in tongue, she is proud and wilful, tyrannising over both Shakespeare and the younger man, 'mortgaged to thy will' — in Elizabethan English 'will' carries the secondary sense of 'sexual organs' : so there is double-talk here, as so often with Shakespeare.

The worst of it, to his mind, is the corruption of his young friend, the loss of innocence and purity :

> Beshrew that heart that makes my heart to groan
> For that deep wound it gives my friend and me !
> Is't not enough to torture me alone,
> But slave to slavery my sweet'st friend must be ?

She is a calculating woman — Shakespeare refers to her 'cunning' — and her enticement of the younger man is part of her hold on the older :

> To tempt me soon to hell, my female evil
> Tempteth my better angel from my side,
> And would corrupt my saint to be a devil,
> Wooing his purity with her four pride.

Remember here the secondary meaning of 'hell' — which meant the female organ to Elizabethans (as still in some quarters today).

Shakespeare sums up his situation :

> Two loves I have, of comfort and despair,
> Which, like two spirits, do suggest me still :
> The better angel is a man right fair,
> The worser spirit a woman coloured ill.

We might pause to appreciate the infallible verbal dexterity with which Shakespeare talks double-talk in verse — as other poets do, too, and people don't notice it. But we are concerned with facts, and here he tells us that since his mistress and the young man have become intimate,

> I guess one angel in another's hell.
> Yet this shall I ne'er know, but live in doubt,
> Till my bad angel fire my good one out.

('Fire' has the secondary meaning of sexual disease.)

Although the affair was a very distracting one. Naturally there were pleasant intervals, as when the musical lady played the virginals to him ; sometimes she would take pity on him and be kind, with her dark eyes, 'black and loving mourners',

> Looking with pretty ruth upon my pain.

It was a humiliating situation with her running after the young Earl, while Shakespeare, older than them both, is left behind :

> So runn'st thou after that which flies from thee,
> Whilst I, thy babe, chase thee far behind.
> But if thou catch thy hope, turn back to me
> And play the mother's part, kiss me, be kind.
> So will I pray that thou mayst have thy will,
> If thou turn back, and my loud crying still.

Southampton was still unmarried — for which Shakespeare reproached him ; and, with his nature, it is not likely that he was emotionally involved : it was Shakespeare who was humiliatingly infatuated.

Sometimes she would consent to go to bed with him, and then go back on the promise she made in bed to keep faith with him. This is the meaning of the lines,

> In act thy bed-vow broke and new faith torn,
> In vowing new hate after new love bearing.

This has often been taken to mean that she was breaking her own marriage-vow ; though this is not the immediate literal meaning, one must not forget Shakespeare's habitual double-talk, with a secondary suggestion. With his characteristic openness of mind ('he was indeed honest, and of an open and free nature' — Ben Jonson) he admitted that he was breaking his own marriage-vow :

> In loving thee thou know'st I am forsworn,
> But thou art twice forsworn, to me love swearing

— and then going back on it. If we look at the situation from the woman's point of view, no doubt it was sometimes a trial ; no wonder she preferred chasing Southampton. (We find later that Shakespeare was six years older than she was, more than nine years older than Southampton ; these simple facts are more than enough to account for his consciousness of his age, about which there has been so much dubious discussion. It also doubled the sense of humiliation, to be an older person chasing a young woman who clearly did not want him.) The Sonnets show that there were quarrels, a reconciliation and a new breach, a final one :

> For all my vows are oaths but to misuse thee,
> And all my honest faith in thee is lost.

He had found no constancy or trust in her, but duplicity and breach of faith ; she was temperamental and spoilt. The young

woman had no love for him, but was occasionally 'kind' in going
to bed with him, as with others.

There was little satisfaction in such a relationship. It was a very
near thing that it had not ruined Shakespeare's friendship with his
young patron — more important to him in every way, except
sexually. The affair had besmirched Shakespeare's reputation — so
again the lady was a character known. He defends himself : other
people are no better :

> For why should others' false adulterate eyes,
> Give salutation to my sportive blood ?

Note again the double meaning of 'adulterate' — it is suggesting
that these people are also adulterous. Shakespeare comes clear, with
the manly affirmation that, in spite of his frailties — notably his
weakness for women :

> No, I am that I am, and they that level
> At my abuses reckon up their own.

His very frankness is endearing ; he makes no excuse for himself ;
he has no moral pretences, he does not hold himself in any high
moral esteem. But with his knowledge of human nature, he knows
that others are no better and does not allow them to condemn him
for 'his sportive blood', or even himself to lose any pleasure for
their condemnation :

> By their rank thoughts my deeds must not be shown.

His own inner condemnation, his ill conscience, is all that matters.
One way and another, the affair drove him to distraction :

> My love is a fever, longing still
> For that which longer nurseth the disease.

Indeed it is like a disease ; his reason is all against it,

> Angry that his prescriptions are not kept.

It is a sick state of mind where one's emotions are in absolute
conflict with one's reason and judgement, and of course it drove
him frantic :

> Past cure I am, now reason is past care,
> And frantic-mad with evermore unrest.

No good could come of it : something should happen to bring it to
an end.

xxxii

It seems to have come to an end quite suddenly ; perhaps a journey away from London wrenched him away from her spell :

> I, sick withal, the help of bath desired
> And thither hied, a sad distempered guest.

This comes in the last two sonnets, about Cupid as god of love, which form a kind of coda in lighter-hearted vein ; though the second and last sonnet of all repeats the reference to

> a bath and helpful remedy
> For men diseased ;

and to himself as

> my mistress' thrall
> Came there for cure.

Is there a double meaning here too ? — had he caught a disease ?

The Sonnets dealing with her end with this. The affair was over. But what an affair it had been ! — of what complexity and subtlety: one may compare it with Benjamin Constant's *Adolphe*. It is stranger than that, for the main subject remains after all not the infatuation with the Dark Lady but the friendship between poet and patron. Thus it is unique : it is no wonder that its inflexions and nuances have never been satisfactorily grasped, any more than the facts behind them worked out and made clear.

For all the agitation and anxiety in this complicated affair there remained the great consolation for a writer — Henry James would agree, though himself incapable of the experience : creative inspiration. Shakespeare was able to see himself and it, even as it was going on, from the outside and as a conclusion to give it the light-hearted, if rueful, coda. That is what genius, a kind of self-observing mirror, can do.

The whole thing was experienced and expressed, rounded up, in those three years. After that there is no further indication of an obsession with a Dark Lady, an infatuation with black eyes, hair, brows. There is no further indication of sonneteering — so evident not only in these poems themselves but in the verse-forms of *Love's Labour's Lost*, which belongs wholly with them and their experience. He had other things to do, far too much on hand once this entanglement was over.

All in all, with his characteristic candour and openness, he has told us everything about the Dark Lady, except her name.

VII

Who the Dark Lady Was

Two or three years later — to be precise, on 13 May 1597 — there came to consult the astrologer, Simon Forman, a young man named William Lanier.[1] He lived in Longditch, Westminster, near the bridge that led to Canon Row, the fashionable quarter near the Court at Whitehall, where peers and grandees lived. He was now twenty-four and had some suit in hand, for he was about to serve in Essex's Islands Voyage — the expedition to the Azores, upon which Southampton served with success in command of the *Garland*.

Four days later, 17 May, Lanier's wife came to consult Forman, who wrote down information about everyone coming his way ; it was necessary for casting figures to forecast what would or might come about, and indispensable that it should be as minute and accurate as possible. She was the daughter of Baptist Bassano and Margaret Johnson — Bassano had been one of the Queen's Italian musicians — and was now twenty-seven : so three years older than her husband. 'She hath had hard fortune in her youth. Her father died when she was young ; the wealth of her father failed before he died and he began to be miserable in his estate.' A second figure cast for her is accompanied by the information that 'she was paramour to my old Lord Hunsdon that was Lord Chamberlain and was maintained in great pride ; being with child, she was for colour married to a minstrel', *i.e.* Lanier.

On 3 June she comes to inquire whether her husband shall have the suit. For herself, 'she seems to be with child of twelve days or weeks — much pain in her left side — but it will hardly stay with her : she hath many false conceptions. He shall have the suit, but first be in despair of it. She was brought up in the county of Kent [that would probably be near the Court at Greenwich] and hath been married four years.' That takes us back to 1593. 'The old Lord Chamberlain kept her longer.' So that must have been from 1589, or before. She would have been born in 1570. 'She was maintained in great pomp. She is high-minded — she hath something in her mind she would have done for her. She hath £40 a year [a good *dot* for those days] and was wealthy to him that married her, in money and jewels. She can hardly keep secret. She was very brown in youth.' Forman never notes this of anyone else :

[1] MS. Ashmole 226.

he means that she was exceptionally dark. 'She hath a son, Henry' — evidently named after the old Lord Chamberlain.

An unknown life begins to unfold before us.

On 16 June she comes again to inquire whether her husband shall come to any preferment before he comes home. On 2 September, before the expedition returned, she puts the question whether she shall be a Lady, *i.e.* of title, and how she shall speed. *[handwritten: astrologer]* Forman now gives us a fuller character sketch of her, based on what she told him, with her high-mindedness. 'She hath been favoured much of her Majesty and of many noblemen, hath had great gifts and been made much of — a nobleman that is dead hath loved her well and kept her. But her husband hath dealt hardly with her, hath spent and consumed her goods. She is now very needy, in debt and it seems for lucre's sake [very strangely, perhaps by some unconscious suggestion, Forman actually wrote 'for *Lucrece* sake'] will be a good fellow, for necessity doth compel. She hath a wart or mole in the pit of the throat or near it.'[1]

There follows Forman's forecast ; this is of less interest to us : we are interested only in the facts. The figure seemed to indicate that she would become a Lady 'or attain to some greater dignity'. Her husband would be 'knighted hardly', *i.e.* doubtfully, and 'get little substance ... It seems he will not live two years after he come home.' It would be interesting to know if this forecast were fulfilled. Elsewhere Forman has an unfavourable comment on the lady and her husband, who had 'gone to sea with the Earl of Essex in hope to be knighted — though there was little cause why he should' He added later : 'he was not knighted, nor yet worthy thereof'.

Forman's interest, always alert where women were concerned, was aroused ; the husband's absence provided an opportunity. An unattached note, difficult to interpret, seems to relate to her. The figure 'shows the woman hath a mind to the quent, but seems she is or will be a harlot. And because ... she useth sodomy.' This sophistication, *à la* Lady Chatterley, was merely what the figure indicated, we must remember. However, on 10 September he puts the question, 'if I go to Lanier [note the disrespectful absence of Mrs.] this night or tomorrow, whether she will receive me, and whether I shall be welcome et halek', that is Forman's regular term for intercourse.

We have information from him as to what happened next day, 11 September. 'A certain gentleman longed to see a gentlewoman

[1] MS. Ashmole 354.

whom he loved [*i.e.* wanted] and desired to halek with.' He set the figure whether it were best to send a messenger to know how she did, and whether she would bid him come to her or no. 'The party sent his servant, by whom she sent word that if his master came he should be welcome. He went and supped with her and stayed all night. She was familiar and friendly to him in all things, but only she would not halek. Yet he felt all parts of her body willingly and kissed her often, but she would not do in any wise. Whereupon he took some displeasure, and so departed friends, but not intending to come at her again in haste.' To this he added, 'but yet ready were friends again afterward — but he never obtained his purpose [he meant at that time]. She was a whore, and dealt evil with him after.'

Forman sounds censorious in his disappointment : a better word would be to say that she was a cocotte.

Six days later, on 17 September, she simply sent for Forman, in her high-handed way.[1] He put the question for himself whether it were best to go. The figure said that she appeared to be afraid, but in fact was not. Another six days passed before he put the question whether to go or no.[2] He had not obeyed her command ; so 'next afternoon she sent her maid to me, and I went with her to her.'

29 October was a very full day for Forman. He went to see the state-opening of Parliament by the Queen in her robes, sword of state carried before her. At the show he stood beside a lady of good name and family, Joan Harington, who made an assignation with him, and at 4 o'clock that afternoon came to him 'and did halek etc. very friendly'.[3] We see how free and easy Elizabethans were apt to be in these matters. Only half an hour before he had put the question whether 'to go to Lanier's this night or no'. She sent both her manservant and maid to fetch him : 'I went with them and stayed all night.'

We are not told whether her husband, Will Lanier, came home. But Forman's relations with Emilia were not purely physical. At the end of 1597 he reminds himself, in the decent obscurity of Latin — in case anyone was prying into his Case-Books — to put the question concerning Lanier's tales as to the invocation of spirits, whether not an incuba (apparently meaning her), 'and whether I shall end it or no'. She was still going a couple of years later, for on 7 January 1600, he sets the question 'to know why Mrs. Lanier sent

[1] MS. Ashmole 226.   [2] MS. Ashmole 354.
[3] MS. Ashmole 226.

for me ; what will follow, and whether she intendeth any more villainy'.[1]

So he, too, had an ill experience with her, an ill opinion of her.

Did she dabble in spells and the invocation of spirits ? There would be nothing improbable in that in the Elizabethan Age. From the valedictory sonnet to Marlowe, Sonnet 86, it is clear that he did :

> Was it his spirit, by spirits taught to write
> Above a mortal pitch, that struck me dead ?
> No, neither he, nor his compeers by night
> Giving him aid, my verse astonishèd.
> He, nor that affable familiar ghost
> Which nightly gulls him with intelligence,
> As victors of my silence cannot boast . . .

We know from *Dr. Faustus* that Marlowe knew the Latin formulas for summoning up the spirits, by which he summoned up Mephistophilis, his 'affable familiar' — in Elizabethan English affable means complaisant, as we might say in 'collusion'.

Now that we know that the Dark Lady's husband — married in this very year 1593 — was another Will, there remains no difficulty in interpreting the two comic Will Sonnets, 135 and 136, which have never been explained and have given rise to acute embarrassment among their commentators — even more confusion, when they hadn't a clue to what they meant. Remember always that 'will' had a naughty secondary sense, meaning sexual parts, to unembarrassed Elizabethans.

> Whoever hath her wish, thou hast thy will,
> And Will to boot, and Will in overplus.

Perfectly clear now : in addition to her own sex, she has Will Lanier's and Will Shakespeare's at her command.

The Sonnets can now be read for the amusement they give, with their characteristic double-talk, as they provided amusement for Southampton, for whom they were written. It is good to think they got some fun out of it, along with the vexation and mistrust, the expense of spirit, the shame (everything was heightened and more coloured in that age.)

> Wilt thou, whose will is large and spacious,
> Not once vouchsafe to hide my will in thine ?
> Shall will in others seem right gracious
> And in my will no fair acceptance shine ?

[1] MS. Ashmole 236.

Again, in Sonnet 136, two Wills are admitted into her's :

> Swear to thy blind soul that I was thy Will ;
> And Will, thy soul knows, is admitted there :

i.e. her husband, in good conscience.

> Will will fulfil the treasure of thy love,
> Ay, fill it full with wills, and my will one.

Hyder Rollins, in the *New Variorum Shakespeare*, has an inkling of the meaning and refers, with some embarrassment, to the 'less pleasant supposed meanings of *will*'. Why 'less pleasant' ? Without them we should not be here.

He asked for answers to his 'unanswerable questions'. Now at last we have them.

VIII

Historic Circumstances

We can now construct the framework of the Dark Lady's life from the documents : they corroborate the account of her in the Sonnets and what Forman tells us about her at every point. She came from a family of Italian musicians at Court. The Bassanos came into England at the end of Henry VIII's reign ; they continued as royal musicians for three or four generations, up to the Civil War.[1] Their name tells us that they came from Bassano in the state of Venice — the documents refer to the first generation of them as 'natives of Venice'. They were a numerous clan and this adds to the difficulty of pinpointing them.

But there is no difficulty about Emilia here : we know her parents. They were Baptist Bassano and Margaret Johnson, who lived together as man and wife, evidently not married. Both were buried in the parish of St. Botolph Bishopsgate, just outside the walls of the City, on the way to Shoreditch where the early theatres were, the 'Theatre' and the 'Curtain', and where so many of the theatre-folk lived. The parish registers record the burials of Baptist Bassano, 'the Queen's musician', on 11 May 1576, and of Margaret Bassano — so she went by his name — on 7 July 1587.[2]

Forman was quite right : Emilia was a girl of only six when her father died. Fortunately we have his will : Baptista Bassany, as the English called them, 'native of Venice and one of the musicians

---

[1] J. Pulver, *A Bibliographical Dictionary of English Music*, 41 foll.
[2] *Registers of St. Botolph Bishopsgate*, transcr. A. W. C. Hallen, I, 277, 295.

of our sovereign lady the Queen's Majesty'.[1] He leaves to 'Emilia Bassany, daughter of the body of Margaret Bassany alias Margaret Johnson, my reputed wife the sum of £100 . . . to be paid at her full age of 21 years or day of marriage'. If Emilia died before this, the sum was to come to her mother, who was to have the keeping of her and her bestowal in marriage. Emilia had a sister Angela, now married to Joseph Holland, gentleman. To these two daughters Bassano left the rents of the three houses and tenements of which he held the lease in the same parish. The mother of the daughters was the executrix ; but, as we have seen, she died in 1587, leaving Emilia, a very dark girl of seventeen.

<u>She cannot have been much older when the Lord Chamberlain took her and made her his mistress.</u> Henry Carey, first Lord Hunsdon, was now an elderly man, some ten years older than his first cousin the Queen. He was the son of her mother's, Anne Boleyn's, elder sister Mary. Mary Boleyn had been for a time Henry VIII's mistress ; when he discarded her, she had been married off to William Carey, a gentleman-in-waiting, esquire of the Body. Their only son was born about 1524 and named after the King. His father died young, and the boy had not much in the way of prospects.

When Anne Boleyn's daughter came to the throne the world opened out for him. From being plain Henry Carey he was at once created a peer ; he was granted manors in Hertfordshire and Kent — be it noted (where he got the manor of Sevenoaks) — and an income to keep up his position. All the Careys were in clover in Elizabeth's time, who favoured her mother's relations as against her father's, whom she didn't like. Leicester used to say of the Careys that 'they were of the Tribe of Dan, and were *Noli-me-tangeres*, implying that they were not to be contested with, for they were indeed of the Queen's near kindred'.[2]

As it happens Hunsdon turned out a good servant of the state ; he was not a clever man — plenty of those at Court — but a soldierly fellow, honest and forthright ; blunt in his language, a great swearer, he could be trusted. The Queen made him Warden of the East Marches, where he spent many years on and off at Berwick as its Governor. In 1570 he squashed the last embers of feudal resistance in the North to the new deal in the South, with a victory over Leonard Dacre with twice Hunsdon's numbers in the

---

[1] Prerog. Court Cant., Prob/11/58, f. 21.
[2] Sir Robert Naunton, *Fragmenta Regalia* (Arber's English Reprints), 17-18.

field. Though the clever ones at Court thought him stupid, he was well enough educated for a soldier and could quote a Latin phrase ; given the oversight of the Borders with considerable authority in Scottish affairs, he was well informed about them, and gave sound and sensible advice.[1]

No Puritan, he had had his own company of players from 1564, a small troupe. It seems that James Burbage — father of Richard, the star-actor of the Lord Chamberlain's Company later, and Shakespeare's fellow — was for a time Hunsdon's man. James Burbage was the builder and creator of the original play-houses outside Bishopsgate, the Theatre and the Curtain. The City authorities were always trying to suppress them. But when, in 1584, the Recorder sent to 'the owner of the Theatre, who was a stubborn fellow', to bind him over, he sent back word that he was Lord Hunsdon's man and would appeal to him.[2] He must have done so and had his support, for he was sure that the court would not bind him, 'being a Councillor's man'. Next year, 1585, Hunsdon became Lord Chamberlain and that proved a blessing to the players : it strengthened their position with his support at Court ; so long as he was alive they could not be suppressed. And at this time he had a lease of the very buildings within Blackfriars, which Burbage later acquired for an indoors theatre.[3]

Hunsdon himself had his residence in Somerset House, but his son lived in Blackfriars. So did Richard Field, Shakespeare's school-fellow, who printed *Venus and Adonis* there in 1593 and *Lucrece* in 1594. Shakespeare would be in and out correcting proofs — it is evident from his reading that he read the books coming from Field's press.[4]

In the crisis of Armada year, 1588, Hunsdon was brought south to take command of the Queen's bodyguard at Tilbury. It would have been about this time, hardly later, that he took Emilia Bassano for his mistress ; for Forman tells us that she was with the old Lord Chamberlain longer than the four years she had been married by 1597.

When the girl was got with child she was married off, 'for colour' — Forman tells us — to a musician, another Will, Lanier. The child she bore was called after the Lord Chamberlain, Henry — as he had been called after his mother's lover, Henry VIII. This

[1] Cf. *Cal. Border Papers*, I and II, *passim*.
[2] *Queen Elizabeth and her Times*, ed. T. Wright, II, 299.
[3] E. K. Chambers, *The Elizabethan Stage*, II, 497 foll.
[4] Cf. my *William Shakespeare: A Biography*, 62, 65.

was in 1593 — at which time Emilia was twenty-three ; her husband was twenty, Southampton would be twenty in October ; Will Shakespeare was twenty-nine, more than half of his life over. These dates are more eloquent than whole volumes of vague conjecture — and more touching : they bring these dead people to life.

There is a most revealing line in one of the last sonnets Shakespeare devoted to her, before the breach :

> If thy unworthiness raised love in me,
> More worthy I to be beloved of thee.

It would seem to indicate that the situation she was in had originally aroused his sympathy. How much the discovery of the facts behind the story deepens our human understanding of it all, after generations of vague conjecture!

The Laniers were another prolific family of royal musicians, who came from France, the neighbourhood of Rouen.[1] They came in a generation later than the Bassanos, from the 1560s ; but they go on a generation later, to reappear after the Civil War at the Court of Charles II. (Nicholas Lanier, who had been Master of the King's Musick to Charles I, was an acquaintance of John Evelyn : a connoisseur of painting as well as music, he bought some of Charles I's pictures, now again at Windsor.) The Laniers were as prolific as the Bassanos. This makes them as difficult to track, but we are helped by the fact that the English names, William and Henry, are rare among them.

We come upon the track of the Lord Chamberlain's boy by Emilia, Henry Lanier. In 1629 he got a place at Court as one of Charles I's musicians for the flutes ; but by 1633 he is dead, another takes his place.[2] He was only forty ; he left a widow and a son, who also became a royal musician — William, named after Emilia's husband, his putative grandfather.

As for Emilia and William, the Dark Lady and Will, her husband, there is no more about them : they fade into the darkness out of which they came.

But after how fortunate an illumination during just those most significant years, lighted by an incredible stroke of luck !

IX

The old Lord Chamberlain died on 23 July 1596. We have his death-bed scene : on 21 July he called his son and heir George to him and asked 'that he would not leave him that night, who before

---

[1] Pulver, 282.   [2] H. C. de Lafontaine, *The King's Musick*, 70, 86, 88.

was determined to watch with him'.[1] The old man was on good terms with his son and all his family : the heir was 'to possess all and whatsoever I shall leave behind me. So I do think you worthy of it, and much more, for I have always found you a kind and loving son.' He wished his son to take on the administration, since he did not wish his wife to be 'troubled with so broken and hard estate as I shall leave . . . I being able to leave her nothing in respect of that which so good a wife to me and mother to you hath deserved.' In the event the Queen provided for her by passing on to her the keepership of Somerset House ; the son went to live in Blackfriars. 'Her Majesty hath sent me sundry gracious promises that, on the word of a prince, she would fully relieve my estate . . . And therefore doubt not but she will bestow mine offices upon you which, if she do, you may be the better to my said poor servants, which I am not able to recompense.' As we have seen, Emilia had been generously provided for three years before, £40 a year with money and jewels. In the event, the Queen gave the office of Lord Chamberlain to Lord Cobham, but he conveniently died next year and the second Lord Hunsdon succeeded to his father's office in 1597, the year in which Emilia so providentially consulted Forman and Will Lanier went on the Islands Voyage (did he serve under Southampton in the *Garland* ?).

Will Shakespeare had also been provided for with the foundation of the Lord Chamberlain's Company, to become so famous, in 1594. Shakespeare's early biographer, Rowe, derived the information from Sir William Davenant — who liked to think that he was a by-blow of William Shakespeare's by his mother, the buxom hostess of the Crown tavern at Oxford, on the way to and from Stratford — that Southampton gave his poet a handsome sum to go through with a purchase he had a mind to.[2] It is generally considered that it was this that enabled him to purchase a share in the Lord Chamberlain's Company. From that moment, the insecure years over, he had a solid foundation : for the rest of his life he remained in closest association with his fellows, as playwright, actor, producer, sharer of the profits. And what a prodigious use he made of the opportunity, of security, independence at last ! No more time for sonneteering . . .

[1] Prerog. Court Cant., Prob/11/88, f. 54.
[2] See E. K. Chambers, *William Shakespeare : A Study of Facts and Problems*, II, 266–7.

In the last sonnets of the Southampton sequence one can see him drawing away, his mind moving forward into the future. The very last of these sonnets, 125, in cool valedictory spirit, expresses gratitude but also asserts independence, poor (as yet) but free :

No, let me be obsequious [faithful] in thy heart,
And take thou my oblation, poor but free,
Which is not mixed with seconds, knows no art
But mutual render, only me for thee.

It is profoundly right that the last note to be sounded, after all the variations of the relationship, should be that of mere human equality.

In 1598 the poem which Marlowe had been writing in rivalry with *Venus and Adonis* and left unfinished at his death, *Hero and Leander*, was at length published. We need not here go into the detail which shows clearly that Southampton was as much the model for Leander as he was for Adonis — though Marlowe's response to the beauty of male youth is of a different character from Shakespeare's, naturally.[1] The publication, no doubt reading it again, brought back Marlowe to mind, for the play that Shakespeare was writing at the time, *As You Like It*, has no less than three references to him. We are concerned here only with that which is relevant to the Sonnets, when Touchstone comes out with, 'it strikes a man more dead than a great reckoning in a little room'. The quarrel in the little tavern at Deptford, according to the inquest, had been over 'le reckoning' : William Shakespeare would have known quite well how Marlowe, his 'dead shepherd', had died. It had happened on 30 May 1593.

Dates are decisive, as well as illuminating, and one cannot get around them.

x

The Identity of Mr. W. H.

And so we find with the last problem, the identification of Mr. W. H., to whom the Sonnets were dedicated. Now that we at length appreciate that the dedication was the publisher's and Mr. W. H. the person who got the manuscripts for him, we see that it is a matter of minor importance : it comes as a coda. All the same, the dates hold the clue.

The Sonnets were not published until 1609, by Thomas Thorpe, who got the manuscripts from 'Mr. W. H.' Southampton's

[1] Cf. for fuller detail chap. IX, 'The Rival Poets', in my *Christopher Marlowe : A Biography*, 165 foll.

mother had died in 1607, leaving her household goods and chattels to her third husband, a much younger man, Sir William Harvey. Now it is common Elizabethan usage to refer to a knight as Mr. (short for Master) — Sir Francis Bacon, for example, is frequently Master Bacon ; the old Countess regularly refers in her letters to Sir Thomas Heneage, her second husband, as Master Heneage. People who do not know Elizabethan usages are unaware of this, but everybody should know that one could never refer to a Lord as Mr.

Next year, 1609, Harvey married a young wife and could hope for posterity. This is why Thorpe in 1609 is wishing him 'all happiness and that eternity promised by our ever-living poet' — that eternity of carrying on the family which Shakespeare promised Southampton in the Sonnets. 'Wisheth the well-wishing adventurer in setting forth, T. T.' is Thorpe's rather rhetorical reference to the craze for the Virginia venture which swept London that same year. Now perhaps we can see that his rather fancy phrase 'to the only begetter' is just publisher's hyperbole, though he had every reason to be grateful to his man, the one and only person who had got the manuscripts. And so have we.

With this, all the 'unanswerable' questions regarding the Sonnets that have bedevilled Shakespeare scholarship for so long are finally answered ; and, as I have said previously along the way to their solution, they cannot be impugned, for they are the answer. But the last key never would have been discovered if it had not been for Simon Forman and the preservation of his case-books, appropriately in the Bodleian. Without that incredible chance, waiting there all along, it would have been lost, for there is nothing about the Lord Chamberlain's Italianate mistress in print.[1] (When we come to think of it, who else would she be ? Who more appropriate ?)

One might think it a small matter, once it has been discovered. But the literary consequences — apart from the practical, such as the scrapping of all editions of the Sonnets hitherto — are great. For literature, there is the establishment of the Sonnets as a homogeneous, integral work of art belonging only to that period in Shakespeare's life. Reading the Sonnets through now for their story, with our new knowledge of persons, characters and events, adds a dimension to the understanding of them — in particular, of the Dark Lady, her

---

[1] The Emilia Lanier who appears as a petitioner in the 1630s (*Cal. S.P. Dom.* 1634-5, 516-17, and foll. vols.) was the widow of Captain Alphonse Lanier, servant to James I.

rather pitiable situation, Shakespeare's sympathy for her in it that first aroused love, then the nature of the older man's infatuation for an equivocal and (emotionally) unresponsive young woman. We see now, with the sympathy of knowledge, that with her experience of life she could hardly be expected to respond.

Again, reading the Sonnets through as a whole, I cannot imagine how ever people managed to miss the overwhelming obviousness that, in their whole argument and character, they are duty-sonnets written by the poet to his patron. This is their very nature and theme — though they became also poems of friendship, a kind of love, not infatuation, as the relationship developed. And a deeper exploration reveals the various sections into which the Sonnets naturally fall, with the experiences they describe, the themes and conceits they develop, the intervals of absence, returns and renewals of contact. If one considers the work now as a whole — with the fresh inspiration it offers for criticism — it will be seen that it has a subtle organisation of its own. It could hardly be more so than if planned — though we may surmise that Shakespeare, like the professional he was, was not without some such idea of what he was working towards, as he went along.

From the point of view of the text, the new information, making clear what was in the dark before, has greatly helped the rendering of the Sonnets into modern English, particularly those concerned with the Dark Lady, so much more difficult than the others. Here I have been able to improve considerably, I hope, on my previous renderings in prose.

It also throws new and revealing lights upon the related works of those years, *Venus and Adonis* and *Lucrece*, the plays, in particular *Love's Labour's Lost* and *A Midsummer Night's Dream* ; and also upon *Hero and Leander* and Marlowe. As things are, all this may take some time to absorb into Shakespeare scholarship. However, the old ingrained habit of literary conjecture, which never could provide any answers or any certainty, had long reached a dead end. It may be hoped that this will provide a new impulse to that scholarship, as all future editions of those works will need to take account of these findings. And, of course, it means rewriting the biography of Shakespeare in the crucial formative period that provided so many new openings in life and art, those significant years of transition to the marvellous creative development that came along with it, and arose partly out of it.

SHAKESPEARE'S SONNETS

Never Before Imprinted

—

At London
By G. Eld for T.T. and are
to be sold by John Wright, dwelling
at Christ Church gate
1609

To the only begetter of

these ensuing sonnets

Mr. W. H. all happiness

and that eternity

promised

by

our ever-living poet

wisheth

the well-wishing

adventurer in

setting

forth

T. T.

SHAKESPEARE'S SONNETS

I

From fairest creatures we desire increase
That thereby beauty's rose might never die,
But as the riper should by time decease
His tender heir might bear his memory :
But thou, contracted to thine own bright eyes,
Feed'st thy light's flame with self-substantial fuel,
Making a famine where abundance lies,
Thyself thy foe, to thy sweet self too cruel.
Thou that art now the world's fresh ornament
And only herald to the gaudy spring,
Within thine own bud buriest thy content
And, tender churl, mak'st waste in niggarding.
   Pity the world, or else this glutton be :
   To eat the world's due, by the grave and thee.

I

We desire that the fairest of creatures may increase that beauty may not die out, but as the older in time dies he may leave an heir to carry on his memory. But you, concerned only with your own beauty, feed the flame of life with self-regarding fuel, making a famine where there is plenty : in this you are being too cruel to yourself. You who are just now coming out into the world, a brilliant ornament in it, are burying what you have to give within yourself. Thus are you wasteful in being so skinflint. Take pity on the world, or else be regarded as a glutton — to eat up what is due to the world by dying childless.

This sonnet offers the reader no difficulty, except perhaps in the meaning of the last line : 'by the grave and thee' contains two ideas in great conciseness — it refers both to Southampton's dying and to his dying childless. I content myself with drawing attention to the internal rhyme in ll. 1 and 4, and the lovely alliteration in f's that carries through much of the sonnet but is particularly concentrated in ll. 6-8.

2

When forty winters shall besiege thy brow
And dig deep trenches in thy beauty's field,
Thy youth's proud livery, so gazed on now,
Will be a tattered weed of small worth held :
Then, being asked where all thy beauty lies,
Where all the treasure of thy lusty days,
To say within thine own deep-sunken eyes
Were an all-eating shame and thriftless praise.
How much more praise deserved thy beauty's use
If thou couldst answer 'This fair child of mine
Shall sum my count and make my old excuse',
Proving his beauty by succession thine !
    This were to be new-made when thou art old
    And see thy blood warm when thou feel'st it cold.

2

When forty winters have gone by and left deep furrows on you, the pride and flourish of your youth, so much admired by the world now, will be a rag of little worth. When asked then, 'where is your beauty now? where is the treasure of your lusty youth?', to answer — 'only within your own sunken eyes' — were a consuming shame and profitless praise. To use your beauty would be more deserving of commendation : if you could answer, 'This fair child speaks for me and makes up my account, a sufficient excuse for my old age', his beauty would be yours still in succession. This were to be new-made when agèd, and see your own blood warm in him when you feel it cold.

No difficulty in meaning, except for the conciseness of l. 12. Notice the double, and paradoxical, use of the word 'livery' in l. 3. It means the distinctive clothes worn by the servants of some great person ; to apply it to the young earl's outward appearance is a characteristically Shake-spearean turn of thought. We learn from the same line that on coming out into the world, at the age of eighteen, the young earl is much 'gazed on'.

3

Look in thy glass and tell the face thou viewest
Now is the time that face should form another,
Whose fresh repair if now thou not renewest
Thou dost beguile the world, unbless some mother.
For where is she so fair whose uneared womb
Disdains the tillage of thy husbandry ?
Or who is he so fond will be the tomb
Of his self-love to stop posterity ?
Thou art thy mother's glass and she in thee
Calls back the lovely April of her prime,
So thou through windows of thine age shall see,
Despite of wrinkles, this thy golden time.
 But if thou live remembered not to be,
 Die single and thine image dies with thee.

3

Look in your glass and tell the face you see that now is the time it should form another ; if you do not renew it, you rob the world and some likely mother of a child. For where is the woman whose unploughed womb would disdain your tillage ? Or who is he so foolish as to bury himself in self-love and halt posterity ? You are the mirror of your mother, and in you she calls back the lovely April of her youth. So you, through your own children, may see again this golden time despite the furrows of age. But if you live your life so as not to be remembered and die single, then your image dies with you.

———

No difficulty, except the Elizabethan word 'uneared' in l. 5, which means unploughed. In his dedication of *Venus and Adonis* to Southampton, Shakespeare again used this country word : 'but if the first heir of my invention prove deformed, I shall be sorry it had so noble a godfather, and never after ear so barren a land, for fear it yield me still so bad a harvest'. In 'husbandry', l. 6, there is the double suggestion of cultivating the soil and marriage. In ll. 9–10 Shakespeare takes characteristically courteous occasion for a salute to his patron's mother, the Countess of Southampton.

4

Unthrifty loveliness, why dost thou spend
Upon thyself thy beauty's legacy ?
Nature's bequest gives nothing but doth lend,
And, being frank, she lends to those are free.
Then, beauteous niggard, why dost thou abuse
The bounteous largess given thee to give ?
Profitless usurer, why dost thou use
So great a sum of sums yet canst not live ?
For, having traffic with thyself alone,
Thou of thyself thy sweet self dost deceive.
Then how, when nature calls thee to be gone,
What acceptable audit canst thou leave ?
    Thy unused beauty must be tombed with thee,
    Which, used, lives the executor to be.

4

Careless of your beauty, why do you spend upon yourself the legacy you have inherited ? Nature does not give outright but lends and, being open-handed, she lends to those who are generous in return. Then why do you abuse the bounteous gifts given you to hand on ? Like a usurer not knowing how to profit by it, why possess such treasures and know not how to use them ? Trafficking with yourself alone, you defraud yourself. When nature calls you to your rest, how can you render up an acceptable account ? Your unused beauty must go profitless into the grave — when, if you use it, it will live in your progeny to take care of your memory.

The conceit that runs all through this sonnet is that of use and usury, profit and interest, so familiar and pressing a theme to Elizabethans. It is carried ingeniously forward and backward to refer to the looks that Southampton has inherited from his mother, the young man's commerce with himself, the account he will render up at his last audit, his state without leaving himself an executor. There are no difficulties in all this: one can only admire the natural ingeniousness of it. Observe the characteristic Shakespearean reflexive conceit in l. 10, 'Thou of thyself thy sweet self dost deceive'.

11

5

Those hours that with gentle work did frame
The lovely gaze where every eye doth dwell
Will play the tyrants to the very same
And that unfair which fairly doth excel :
For never-resting time leads summer on
To hideous winter and confounds him there ;
Sap checked with frost and lusty leaves quite gone,
Beauty o'ersnowed and bareness everywhere.
Then, were not summer's distillation left,
A liquid prisoner pent in walls of glass,
Beauty's effect with beauty were bereft,
Nor it, nor no remembrance what it was :
    But flowers distilled, though they with winter meet,
    Lose but their show ; their substance still lives sweet.

5

Those hours that gently shaped the lovely spectacle everyone now gazes upon will prove tyrant and deprive it of its loveliness in time to come. For summer leads on to winter, the sap of life is frosted, leaves fall, beauty is touched with snow, bareness all round. Then, were there no distillation of summer left, like rose-water imprisoned in a glass, what beauty can create would be lost with itself, leaving no remembrance even of what it was. But if flowers are distilled, even though they come to their end, they lose but their external form ; their substance continues sweet.

———

This sonnet follows up another conceit, which Shakespeare seems to have derived from Sidney's *Arcadia* : 'have you ever seen a pure rose-water kept in a crystal glass ? How fine it looks, how sweet it smells while that beautiful glass imprisons it ? Break the prison, and let the water take his own course, doth it not embrace dust and lose all his former sweetness and fairness ? Truly, so are we — if we have not the stay, rather than the restraint, of crystalline marriage.'

The idea of the distillation of summer is carried forward into *A Midsummer-Night's Dream*, I. i. 76-8 :

> But earthlier happy is the rose distilled
> Than that which withering on the virgin thorn
> Grows, lives and dies in single blessedness :

where it is again a reference to Southampton's single state, on the occasion of his mother's marriage to Sir Thomas Heneage, 2 May 1594. In l. 1 'hours' is a disyllable, and should be pronounced, as it is spelt in the original text, 'howers'.

6

Then let not winter's ragged hand deface
In thee thy summer ere thou be distilled :
Make sweet some vial ; treasure thou some place
With beauty's treasure, ere it be self-killed.
That use is not forbidden usury
Which happies those that pay the willing loan ;
That's for thyself to breed another thee,
Or, ten times happier, be it ten for one.
Ten times thyself were happier than thou art
If ten of thine ten times refigured thee :
Then what could death do, if thou shouldst depart,
Leaving thee living in posterity ?
    Be not self-willed, for thou art much too fair
    To be death's conquest and make worms thine heir.

6

Then let not rough winter deface your summer's prime before you leave some essence of yourself : distil yourself into some vial, enrich some place with your beauty, let it not be destroyed by you. That usury is not forbidden which makes those happy to pay the increase on it willingly ; that is, for you to breed another like yourself, or — ten times better — ten like you. It were better for you if there were ten of you to multiply your image ; what could death do then, if you were taken away, leaving you alive in your posterity ? Do not be self-willed : you are too fair to be extinguished utterly by death, with only worms for heir.

This sonnet is a kind of antiphon to the one preceding, echoing the images of summer and winter, of summer's distillation and the vial. It also takes up the idea of usury that dominates Sonnet 4, and plays on the statutory limitation on usury at the time to ten per cent. Evidently composed along with these sonnets, it offers a kind of conclusion, and we may regard Sonnets 1-6 as hanging close together in time, forming a first section, a prelude.

7

Lo, in the orient when the gracious light
Lifts up his burning head, each under eye
Doth homage to his new-appearing sight,
Serving with looks his sacred majesty,
And having climbed the steep-up heavenly hill,
Resembling strong youth in his middle age,
Yet mortal looks adore his beauty still,
Attending on his golden pilgrimage ;
But when from highmost pitch with weary car,
Like feeble age, he reeleth from the day,
The eyes, 'fore duteous, now converted are
From his low tract and look another way :
   So thou, thyself out-going in thy noon,
   Unlooked-on diest unless thou get a son.

7

When first the light of the sun appears in the east, earthly eyes do homage to his new appearance ; and when, like a strong youth in his prime, he climbs up the hill of heaven, mortals still worship his glory, attending on his golden pilgrimage. But when from his zenith he reels down the sky at evening, like feeble age, men's eyes, before dutiful, turn away from him. So, if having outstripped your prime you die, you will die unregarded — unless you get a son.

———

This rather far-fetched and not particularly inspired sonnet — it seems to me to reflect Spenser — reads like a new beginning and starts a new section. The imagery of the sun derives from Shakespeare's classical reading, particularly Ovid. In l. 2 'under eye' means sub-solar, *i.e.* earthly, eye ; in l. 5 'steep-up' means almost vertical, as at midday. The only difficulty is the phrase in l. 13, 'thyself out-going in thy noon', which has the sense of going beyond or outstripping. Most interesting is to note the closeness of l. 14 to *Venus and Adonis*, l. 168 : 'Thou wast begot : to get it is thy duty'. Here is another indication of date : *Venus and Adonis*, published in 1593, would have been written in 1592–3.

8

Music to hear, why hear'st thou music sadly ?
Sweets with sweets war not, joy delights in joy :
Why lov'st thou that which thou receiv'st not gladly,
Or else receiv'st with pleasure thine annoy ?
If the true concord of well-tunèd sounds,
By unions married, do offend thine ear,
They do but sweetly chide thee who confounds
In singleness the parts that thou shouldst bear.
Mark how one string, sweet husband to another,
Strikes each in each by mutual ordering,
Resembling sire and child and happy mother
Who, all in one, one pleasing note do sing :
   Whose speechless song, being many, seeming one,
   Sings this to thee : 'Thou single wilt prove none'.

8

You who are music to hear, why are you sad to hear it ? Joy does not conflict with joy : why do you love that which you receive not gladly, or else receive with pleasure what hurts you ? If the harmony of well-tuned sounds married together offends your ear, they reproach you for keeping in unison the several parts that you should bear. Mark how one string, wedded to another, strikes each one in mutual order — just like father, mother, child, who sing together all in one. Their wordless voices, together sounding one, sing this message to you : 'Single, you will come to nothing'.

————

This sonnet changes the metaphor to music and tackles the young man from another side. We know that Shakespeare loved music, but Southampton's attitude is described here as ambivalent. If he liked it, nevertheless it disturbed him. Well it might, for its harmony of sounds married together was a reproach to his single state : such is the theme, ingeniously worked out. The only difficulty is in the conciseness of the phrase in the last line, 'thou single wilt prove none', which relates to the popular phrase, 'one and none is all one'. Observe in l. 8 the characteristic suggestiveness of the word 'bear', *i.e.* to bear or carry a part, to bear the burden, in music or in life, to bear children. Years later, something of l. 14, long dormant in Shakespeare's mind, came to the surface again in *The Phoenix and the Turtle*, l. 28 : 'Number there in love was slain'.

9

Is it for fear to wet a widow's eye
That thou consum'st thyself in single life ?
Ah, if thou issueless shalt hap to die
The world will wail thee like a mateless wife ;
The world will be thy widow and still weep
That thou no form of thee hast left behind,
When every private widow well may keep,
By children's eyes, her husband's shape in mind.
Look, what an unthrift in the world doth spend
Shifts but his place, for still the world enjoys it ;
But beauty's waste hath in the world an end
And, kept unused, the user so destroys it.
   No love toward others in that bosom sits
   That on himself such murd'rous shame commits.

9

Is it for fear of leaving a widow to grieve for you that you consume your life in the single state ? But, if you die without children, the world will lament you and grieve that you have left no pattern of yourself behind — when every private widow may keep her husband's shape in mind through their children. What a waster in the world throws away is but handing it over to someone else, for still the world enjoys it ; but the waste of beauty makes a final end for, if it is not put to use, it is destroyed with and by its possessor. There is no love towards others in the bosom of one who commits such a crime.

This pushes forward the theme now from another side, putting another aspect of the case. In l. 4 the original phrase is 'makeless wife' : cf. the medieval carol, 'I sing of a maiden that is makeless'. The modern equivalent of this is 'mateless'. Observe the alliteration in w's that runs through practically the whole sonnet and fortifies it. Ll. 11-12 have an obvious parallel in Marlowe's *Hero and Leander*, I. 328 : 'Beauty alone is lost, too warily kept'. And this, considering what we now know about the nature of this poem and its relation to Southampton, is significant. Cf. my *William Shakespeare*, pp. 175-7.

10

For shame deny that thou bear'st love to any
Who for thyself art so unprovident.
Grant, if thou wilt, thou art beloved of many,
But that thou none lov'st is most evident :
For thou art so possessed with murd'rous hate
That 'gainst thyself thou stick'st not to conspire,
Seeking that beauteous roof to ruinate
Which to repair should be thy chief desire.
O, change thy thought, that I may change my mind !
Shall hate be fairer lodged than gentle love ?
Be, as thy presence is, gracious and kind,
Or to thyself at least kind-hearted prove :
    Make thee another self, for love of me,
    That beauty still may live in thine or thee.

How can you claim to be loving towards others when you are so improvident of yourself? Grant that there are many who love you, still it is clear that you love none : for you are possessed with hate, to conspire against yourself like this, bringing ruin upon your house when it should be your chief desire to shore it up. Reverse your course, that I may change my mind of you ! Should hate be lodged in a fairer shell than love itself? Be true to yourself, be gracious and kind, as your nature is, or at least be kind to yourself. Make you another self, for love of me, that your beauty may live on in you and yours.

In this sonnet Shakespeare speaks out for the first time in his own person ; for the first time he says 'I', and 'Make thee another self, for love of me'. Evidently his emotion has been touched, and this can be felt in the more intimate and personal language of the poem. We must not exclude the possibility that the poet had been called in by the young Earl's mother to aid her in her campaign of persuading her son to marry and carry on his house. This is the point of ll. 7-8 : it was Southampton's duty to repair the fortunes of his family, damaged by his father's extravagance, jeopardised by its Catholicism, and make its future safe.

One notes the tone of polite exaggeration, almost in inverted commas, by now a kind of banter, almost a game between them. For now Shakespeare's own feelings are becoming engaged : *he* has been caught by the young peer's charm.

From the point of view of dating it is important to note that l. 7 has close parallels in Shakespeare's first two comedies : cf. *The Comedy of Errors*, III. ii. 4, 'Shall love, in building, grow so ruinous' ; and *The Two Gentlemen of Verona*, V. iv. 9, 'Lest, growing ruinous, the building fall'.

11

As fast as thou shalt wane so fast thou grow'st
In one of thine from that which thou departest,
And that fresh blood which youngly thou bestow'st
Thou may'st call thine when thou from youth convertest.
Herein lives wisdom, beauty, and increase,
Without this, folly, age, and cold decay :
If all were minded so the times should cease
And threescore year would make the world away.
Let those whom nature hath not made for store,
Harsh, featureless and rude, barrenly perish :
Look, whom she best endowed she gave the more,
Which bounteous gift thou shouldst in bounty cherish :
  She carved thee for her seal, and meant thereby
  Thou shouldst print more, not let that copy die.

II

As fast as you wane so will you grow in a child of yours, from that which you planted : the fresh blood you gave you may still call yours when youth departs. This is wisdom, beauty, and increase : without it, folly, age, decay. If all were minded like you the world would come to an end in man's threescore years. Let those whom nature has not made to breed from — harsh-featured and ugly — perish without offspring : consider, to whom she gave so much she gave even more : the gifts she gave you should multiply. She made you for her seal, intending that you should print more from it, not let the pattern die.

———

Little comment is necessary, except that the word 'departest' in l. 2 offers some difficulty. With the Elizabethans it had the secondary sense of parting with, or giving away : hence my rendering. We have the authority of the Psalmist for holding that 'the days of our age are three-score years and ten'. The Psalms are constantly reflected throughout Shakespeare, most often in the Prayer Book version, which he would have heard in church all his life.

12

When I do count the clock that tells the time
And see the brave day sunk in hideous night,
When I behold the violet past prime
And sable curls all silvered o'er with white,
When lofty trees I see barren of leaves,
Which erst from heat did canopy the herd,
And summer's green all girded up in sheaves
Borne on the bier with white and bristly beard :
Then of thy beauty do I question make
That thou among the wastes of time must go,
Since sweets and beauties do themselves forsake
And die as fast as they see others grow :
    And nothing 'gainst Time's scythe can make defence
    Save breed, to brave him when he takes thee hence.

12

When I count the clock and see bright day sunk into night, when
I behold the violet withering or dark curls streaked with silver, when
I see the trees stripped of their leaves, which earlier sheltered the
herd from the heat, and summer's green corn girded up in sheaves
and borne on the wagon white and bearded — then, thinking of
you, I fear that you must go along with time's waste, since all
lovely things die as fast as they see others grow to take their place.
There is no defence against time save to breed, against the day when
you are taken away.

————

Here is Shakespeare the countryman born and bred. The pastoral picture
of ll. 5-8 suggests that this was written in the country after the barley-
harvest. Notice for dating that the collocation of shade and canopy
appears in *3 Henry VI*, II. v. 42-5 :

> Gives not the hawthorn bush a sweeter shade
> To shepherds, looking on their silly sheep,
> Than doth a rich embroidered canopy
> To kings ?

While ll. 7-8 have a close parallel in *A Midsummer-Night's Dream*, II. i.
94-5 :

> the green corn
> Hath rotted ere his youth attained a beard.

13

O, that you were yourself ! but, love, you are
No longer yours than you yourself here live :
Against this coming end you should prepare
And your sweet semblance to some other give.
So should that beauty which you hold in lease
Find no determination : then you were
Yourself again, after yourself's decease,
When your sweet issue your sweet form should bear.
Who lets so fair a house fall to decay,
Which husbandry in honour might uphold
Against the stormy gusts of winter's day
And barren rage of death's eternal cold ?
   O, none but unthrifts : dear my love, you know
   Yon had a father : let your son say so.

13

O, that you were yourself! but, love, you are no longer yours than you remain alive : against this inevitable end you should take steps by handing on your form and semblance to another. Thus should that beauty of which you have but a lease not come to an end : thus, after your death, you would live again in the form of your offspring. Who lets so fine a house fall into ruin, when honour itself in marriage might uphold it against the storms of winter, against age and barren death ? None but wasters. My love, you yourself had a father : let your son say as much.

This sonnet marks a second stage in the growth of Shakespeare's feelings : the youth is addressed as 'love' and 'dear my love'. In l. 10, once more 'husbandry' is used in both senses and again Southampton's duty not to let his house fall into decay is enforced — the more compellingly for the reference, in the last couplet, to Southampton's dead father : all now rests on the son to continue the house.

Observe again the close parallel with *Venus and Adonis*, ll. 171 foll. :

> Upon the earth's increase why shouldst thou feed,
> Unless the earth with thy increase be fed ?
> By law of nature thou art bound to breed,
> That thine may live when thou thyself art dead ;
> And so, in spite of death, thou dost survive,
> In that thy likeness still is left alive.

14

Not from the stars do I my judgment pluck,
And yet methinks I have astronomy,
But not to tell of good or evil luck,
Of plagues, of dearths, or seasons' quality ;
Nor can I fortune to brief minutes tell,
Pointing to each his thunder, rain and wind,
Or say with princes if it shall go well,
By oft predict that I in heaven find.
But from thine eyes my knowledge I derive,
And, constant stars, in them I read such art
As — truth and beauty shall together thrive
If from thyself to store thou wouldst convert ;
    Or else of thee this I prognosticate :
    Thy end is truth's and beauty's doom and date.

14

I do not judge by the stars, though I have astronomy enough, but not to tell fortunes, or foretell plagues, dearths, or the weather. Nor can I say from minute to minute what the weather will hold, thunder, rain or wind ; or prophesy how it will go with princes, predict by frequent portents what I find in the heavens. I derive my knowledge from your eyes : they are my constant stars, in which I read such a lesson as that truth and beauty will thrive together if only you would turn from yourself to breeding. Otherwise my prophecy is that your end is that of truth and beauty.

———

After all the comparisons, metaphors, images, turns of thought we have had — the seasons, summer and winter, the green corn and the corn white unto the harvest, the concord of music, the looking-glass, the vial, the seal and its imprint — Shakespeare thinks of yet another variation for his theme, on astronomy. The suggestion is thought to come from his reading of Sidney. The age was much given to astrology, and the 1590s in particular to prognostications and almanacs with their forecasts. This sonnet has the first reference to the plague that raged in these years 1592 and 1593. L. 9 is closely paralleled in *Love's Labour's Lost*, of 1593–4, IV. iii. 350 : 'From women's eyes this doctrine I derive'.

15

When I consider every thing that grows
Holds in perfection but a little moment,
That this huge stage presenteth nought but shows
Whereon the stars in secret influence comment ;
When I perceive that men as plants increase,
Cheered and checked even by the self-same sky,
Vaunt in their youthful sap, at height decrease,
And wear their brave state out of memory :
Then the conceit of this inconstant stay
Sets you most rich in youth before my sight,
Where wasteful Time debateth with Decay,
To change your day of youth to sullied night :
    And all in war with Time for love of you,
    As he takes from you, I engraft you new.

15

When I consider that every thing that grows has but a brief moment
of perfection, that the world is but a stage upon whose shows the
stars exert their influence secretly ; when I observe that men increase
like plants, nourished or checked by these same skies, flaunt themselves in the sap of youth, after achieving their full height begin to
decline, so that their brave prime vanishes out of mind : then the
thought of this unceasing change brings your youth richly before
my eyes, where wasteful time combines with decay to change the
daytime of your youth to dark night : engaged in my war with
Time for love of you, as he takes from you so I renew you in my
verse.

This sonnet marks a further stage in the progress of Shakespeare's affection : the last couplet is the first adumbration of the theme of the immortality the poet will confer on the young man — as he did — by his verse.
L. 3 gives us Shakespeare's first reference to the world as a stage, with its
reflection of his profession, of which we shall hear a great deal more as
the sonnets go on. L. 12 has a parallel in *Richard III*, IV. iv. 16 : 'Hath
dimmed your infant morn to agèd night'.

16

But wherefore do not you a mightier way
Make war upon this bloody tyrant, Time?
And fortify yourself in your decay
With means more blessèd than my barren rhyme?
Now stand you on the top of happy hours,
And many maiden gardens, yet unset,
With virtuous wish would bear your living flowers,
Much liker than your painted counterfeit :
So should the lines of life that life repair,
Which this time's pencil, or my pupil pen,
Neither in inward worth nor outward fair,
Can make you live yourself in eyes of men.
  To give away yourself keeps yourself still ;
  And you must live, drawn by your own sweet skill.

16

But why do you not take a more effective way of defeating time? And fortify yourself against decay by better means than my barren verse? Now you stand at the meridian of your day, and many virginal gardens, as yet not planted, would willingly bear your living flowers, much more like you than your painted portrait. So should the living lineaments of you bring you to mind as neither your portrait nor my pen, describing outward appearance or inner worth, can make you live in men's eyes. To give yourself away is a means of preserving yourself : you can then continue, drawn by your own best means.

Southampton was painted about this time : we have a Hilliard miniature of him from the period of the Sonnets. This perhaps suggested the comparison, the figure, that runs through this poem; the phrase in l. 10, 'this time's pencil' may be a specific reference to Hilliard. Ll. 10-11 offer some difficulty through the conciseness of their expression, and there are disputed interpretations of their punctuation and meaning. I give what I take to be the sense of them. L. 14 reflects a line from Sidney's *Arcadia* : 'With his sweet skill my skilless youth he drew'.

17

Who will believe my verse in time to come
If it were filled with your most high deserts ?
Though yet heaven knows it is but as a tomb
Which hides your life and shows not half your parts.
If I could write the beauty of your eyes
And in fresh numbers number all your graces,
The age to come would say, 'This poet lies :
Such heavenly touches ne'er touched earthly faces'.
So should my papers, yellowed with their age,
Be scorned like old men of less truth than tongue,
And your true rights be termed a poet's rage
And stretchèd metre of an antique song :
    But were some child of yours alive that time,
    You should live twice, in it and in my rhyme.

17

Who will believe my verse in time to come if it were filled with your great deserts ? — though it but conceals your life and portrays not half your gifts. If I could describe the beauty of your eyes and number all your graces, the next age would not believe me and would say that such heavenly touches never graced earthly countenances. And my writings, yellow then with age, would be scorned like babbling old men, and untruthful : your due praise would be termed a poet's fantasy, the forced strains of an old song. But were some child of yours alive then, you should have a double life, in it and in my verse.

———

This rather conventional sonnet offers no difficulties. Perhaps I may point out that 'deserts' in l. 2 rhymes with 'parts' in l. 4, since in earlier days 'er' was regularly pronounced 'ar', as in serjeant or clerk (in England) today.

18

Shall I compare thee to a summer's day ?
Thou art more lovely and more temperate :
Rough winds do shake the darling buds of May,
And summer's lease hath all too short a date :
Sometime too hot the eye of heaven shines,
And often is his gold complexion dimmed ;
And every fair from fair sometime declines,
By chance or nature's changing course untrimmed.
But thy eternal summer shall not fade,
Nor lose possession of that fair thou ow'st ;
Nor shall death brag thou wander'st in his shade,
When in eternal lines to time thou grow'st :
  So long as men can breathe, or eyes can see,
  So long lives this, and this gives life to thee.

18

Shall I compare you to a summer's day ? You are more gracious
and even tempered. Rough winds shake the buds of May, and
summer is all too short ; sometimes the sun is too hot, or often is
clouded over ; everything that is fair loses its beauty, by chance or
in the course of nature coarsened. But your eternal summer shall
not fade, nor lose the beauty that belongs to it ; nor shall death
boast possession of you, when in eternal verse you grow one with
time. So long as men can breathe, or eyes can see, so long will this
live, giving you immortality. *everlasting life*

This first of the Sonnets to become very famous sets a difficult problem in
turning it into prose ; for the most part one can only repeat its language,
perfectly direct and straightforward : no problems of interpretation.
One can but notice the inspired nature of the poem : it is the certainty of
love, that brings with it Shakespeare's confidence in the immortality of
his verse. Though a convention with Renaissance poets, it was in this
case prophetically justified.

19

Devouring Time, blunt thou the lion's paws,
And make the earth devour her own sweet brood ;
Pluck the keen teeth from the fierce tiger's jaws,
And burn the long-lived phoenix in her blood ;
Make glad and sorry seasons as thou fleet'st,
And do whate'er thou wilt, swift-footed Time,
To the wide world and all her fading sweets :
But I forbid thee one most heinous crime —
O, carve not with thy hours my love's fair brow,
Nor draw no lines there with thine antique pen ;
Him in thy course untainted do allow
For beauty's pattern to succeeding men.
    Yet do thy worst, old Time : despite thy wrong,
    My love shall in my verse ever live young.

19

Time that devours all, blunt the lion's paws, and make the earth consume her creatures ; take away the tiger's sharp tooth, and let the phoenix be burned alive in her ashes. Swift Time, make happy or sad seasons as you fly, and do what you will to the world and all its fading things of beauty. But I forbid you one crime — mark not my love's brow with your traces, nor draw your lines upon it : allow him to go unscathed, for a pattern of beauty to succeeding generations. Yet, do your worst : despite Time's injury, my love shall live ever young in my verse.

———

This somewhat laboured poem, developing an Elizabethan commonplace, is an antiphon to the preceding, thought up as a kind of consequence to that inspired sonnet. Not all a poet's verse can be expected to be inspired. However, the animal imagery has its quaint curiosity, and reminds one of the animal-woodcuts of the time, Topsell's for instance. And Shakespeare's concern with Time, as a destroyer of youth and beauty, is a fundamental theme of the Southampton sonnets. Hyder Rollins observes, *New Variorum Edition of Shakespeare. The Sonnets*, ll. 52-3 : 'it seems worth noting that the word *time* is used seventy-eight times in 1-126 and not once in the remaining sonnets. Rearrangers have not always observed this fact.'

20

A woman's face with Nature's own hand painted
Hast thou, the master-mistress of my passion ;
A woman's gentle heart, but not acquainted
With shifting change, as is false women's fashion ;
An eye more bright than theirs, less false in rolling,.
Gilding the object whereupon it gazeth ;
A man in hue, all hues in his controlling,
Which steals men's eyes and women's souls amazeth.
And for a woman wert thou first created,
Till Nature, as she wrought thee, fell a-doting,
And by addition me of thee defeated,
By adding one thing to my purpose nothing ;
　　But since she pricked thee out for women's pleasure,
　　Mine be thy love, and thy love's use their treasure.

20

You have a woman's face, with Nature's own colouring, you who
are the master-mistress of my love ; a woman's gentle heart, but
not changeable as is the way with women ; an eye brighter than
theirs, more sincere, lighting up the object it looks upon. A man in
complexion, all complexions at his command, which attracts men's
eyes as much as it steals women's hearts. And for a woman were
you first intended, till Nature slipped up in making you and, by
adding one thing of no use to me, defrauded me of you. But since
she equipped you for women's pleasure, let them have it, so long as
I may have your love.

———

This crucial sonnet gives the key to the nature of Shakespeare's love for
the young man, and shows that it was not homosexual. He does not
want to possess him physically : he is defeated by Southampton's being
of the male sex. If only he were a woman, as he is like one in his youthful
appearance, Shakespeare repines ! Southampton is portrayed as a feminine
youth with something of the qualities of both sexes ; and this in fact was
the case : ambivalent in his youth, there is some evidence of his response
to both sexes, even after his somewhat belated marriage.

It is not worth commenting on the vast amount of nonsense this sonnet
has given rise to, when it is perfectly clear what it says and what it means.
The pun in l. 13 is meant to be enjoyed.

21

So is it not with me as with that Muse,
Stirred by a painted beauty to his verse,
Who heaven itself for ornament doth use
And every fair with his fair doth rehearse,
Making a couplement of proud compare,
With sun and moon, with earth and sea's rich gems,
With April's first-born flowers, and all things rare
That heaven's air in this huge rondure hems.
O, let me, true in love, but truly write,
And then believe me, my love is as fair
As any mother's child, though not so bright
As those gold candles fixed in heaven's air :
   Let them say more that like of hearsay well ;
   I will not praise that purpose not to sell.

I am not like that poet, inspired to write by a painted beauty, who calls upon heaven itself for decoration, adduces everything lovely for comparison, sun and moon, earth and sea, April flowers, everything rare in the world. True in love, let me but write the truth : my love is as fair as any mother's child, though not so bright as the stars. Let them say more that prefer rumour : I will not cry up what I do not propose to sell.

––––––––

It would be pleasant if we could identify a specific poet — or poem — to whom this refers. But imagery of this kind is generic to Elizabethan love-poetry, cf. Spenser's *Amoretti* for a close example, or Sidney's *Astrophil and Stella*. It would indeed be piquant if it were intended to refer to the latter, and to the famous Stella (Penelope, Lady Rich) as the 'painted beauty'. But there is no knowing about that. L. 8 : observe the internal rhyme 'air' with 'rare' : Shakespeare had that obvious first sign of the born poet, spontaneous facility in rhyming. L. 14 is reflected in *Love's Labour's Lost*, IV. iii. 240, 'To things of sale a seller's praise belongs'.

22

My glass shall not persuade me I am old,
So long as youth and thou are of one date ;
But when in thee time's furrows I behold
Then look I death my days should expiate.
For all that beauty that doth cover thee
Is but the seemly raiment of my heart,
Which in thy breast doth live, as thine in me :
How can I then be older than thou art ?
O therefore, love, be of thyself so wary
As I, not for myself, but for thee will,
Bearing thy heart, which I will keep so chary
As tender nurse her babe from faring ill.
    Presume not on thy heart when mine is slain :
    Thou gav'st me thine not to give back again.

22

When I look in the glass I shall not be persuaded that I am old, so long as you are young ; but when I see time's furrows in you, then I expect death to pay the score of my days. For all your external beauty is but the garment of my heart, which lives in your breast, as yours in mine : how can I then be older than you ? Then, love, be as careful of yourself as I will be of you — not for myself, but since I have your heart, which I will keep as tenderly as a nurse keeps her babe from harm. Do not expect your heart back when I am dead : you gave me yours not to give back again.

———

The new image of this sonnet is that of an exchange of hearts between Shakespeare and his young friend : the assumption is therefore that the latter returns Shakespeare's affection. We observe, after the conventional character of the preceding sonnet, the intimate language of this, which betokens a further progress in their relations. The psychological interest of the poem is obvious — with the older man trying to persuade himself against the difference of age between them. In this year 1592 Shakespeare was twenty-eight, for an Elizabethan no longer young ; Southampton was not yet nineteen. Yet we observe a certain tutorial sentiment in ll. 11-12, as if Shakespeare felt himself *in loco parentis*. L. 7 has a close parallel in *Love's Labour's Lost*, V. ii. 825, 'my heart is in thy breast'.

23

As an unperfect actor on the stage
Who with his fear is put beside his part,
Or some fierce thing replete with too much rage,
Whose strength's abundance weakens his own heart :
So I, for fear of trust, forget to say
The perfect ceremony of love's rite,
And in mine own love's strength seem to decay,
O'ercharged with burden of mine own love's might.
O, let my books be then the eloquence
And dumb presagers of my speaking breast,
Who plead for love and look for recompense
More than that tongue that more hath more expressed.
    O, learn to read what silent love hath writ :
    To hear with eyes belongs to love's fine wit.

23

Like an imperfect actor on the stage who is put out of his part with fright, or is too much moved with passion and so weakens his effect : so I, fearing to trust myself, forget to give the full and proper expression of devotion due to love, and filled with too much feeling appear to falter and fail. Let my poems then speak up for me, who plead for love and look for recompense greater than that tongue that has more fully expressed greater ardours. Learn to read then what silent love has written : to hear with one's eyes is a fine point of wit in love.

This sonnet gives us Shakespeare's first extended reference to his own profession as actor, and very effective use he makes of it for a comparison to express his own natural diffidence in the relationship with the young peer. We may infer from it, too, that few words had passed between them on the subject, and that Shakespeare's chief appeal to Southampton was with and through his poems, his 'books', and that so far it was rather a 'silent love'. Only l. 12 presents any difficulty, though the sense is clear enough.

24

Mine eye hath played the painter and hath stelled
Thy beauty's form in table of my heart ;
My body is the frame wherein 'tis held,
And perspective it is best painter's art.
For through the painter must you see his skill
To find where your true image pictured lies,
Which in my bosom's shop is hanging still
That hath his windows glazèd with thine eyes.
Now see what good turns eyes for eyes have done :
Mine eyes have drawn thy shape, and thine for me
Are windows to my breast, where-through the sun
Delights to peep, to gaze therein on thee :
    Yet eyes this cunning want to grace their art,
    They draw but what they see, know not the heart.

24

My eye has played the painter and limned your form upon my heart ; my body is the frame of the picture : it is the best painter's art to give it perspective and depth. Through the painter's skill you must look to find where your true image lies depicted : it hangs in my breast like a picture in a shop, whose windows are your eyes. See what good turns eyes have done for each other : mine have drawn your image, and yours are windows into my breast, through which the sun may peep to gaze on you there. Yet eyes lack this knowledge : they draw only what they see, they do not know the heart.

––––––––

A rather far-fetched conceit in the Elizabethan manner, yet the sincerity shines through the artifice. It reveals Shakespeare becoming more cultivated, with life in London and introduction into the circle of Southampton House.

25

Let those who are in favour with their stars
Of public honour and proud titles boast,
Whilst I, whom fortune of such triumph bars,
Unlooked for joy in that I honour most.
Great princes' favourites their fair leaves spread
But as the marigold at the sun's eye,
And in themselves their pride lies burièd,
For at a frown they in their glory die.
The painful warrior famousèd for fight,
After a thousand victories once foiled,
Is from the book of honour razèd quite,
And all the rest forgot for which he toiled :
    Then happy I, that love and am beloved
    Where I may not remove nor be removed.

25

Let those who are favoured by fortune boast of public honours and titles, while I, deprived of such things by birth and circumstance, take unlooked-for joy in what I honour most. The favourites of princes spread their glory, like the marigold only when the sun shines on them ; their pride dies in them, for at a frown they are cast away. The famous warrior, after all his battles once caught out, is razed from the book of honour and all his services forgotten. How fortunate them am I to love and be beloved where I may neither change nor be rejected.

This extremely revealing sonnet has a double importance for us. First, it reveals Shakespeare's feelings about the restricted circumstances of his birth and fortune. Second, it refers to Sir Walter Ralegh's fall from favour and disgrace, which was the sensation of the summer of 1592. The very phrases closely describe Ralegh's situation and personality : the emphasis on his services and his toil — he can 'toil terribly', Sir Robert Cecil wrote of him at just this juncture. Ralegh himself wrote, 'once amiss hath bereaved me of all' — a phrase reflected in 'once foiled', cf. my *Ralegh and the Throckmortons*, p. 163. In l. 9 'painful' means painstaking, hardworking : a well-recognised characteristic of Ralegh's.

26

Lord of my love, to whom in vassalage
Thy merit hath my duty strongly knit,
To thee I send this written ambassage
To witness duty, not to show my wit :
Duty so great, which wit so poor as mine
May make seem bare, in wanting words to show it,
But that I hope some good conceit of thine
In thy soul's thought, all naked, will bestow it :
Till whatsoever star that guides my moving
Points on me graciously with fair aspect
And puts apparel on my tattered loving
To show me worthy of thy sweet respect :
   Then may I dare to boast how I do love thee,
   Till then not show my head where thou mayst prove me.

26

Lord of my love, whose own merits have much strengthened my sense of duty, I send this token of my service rather than to vaunt any wit of mine. My wit is indeed bare to express so bounden a duty, but that I hope your good opinion will commend it, all naked as it is, in your inner thoughts, till such time as my fortune takes a more favourable turn and clothes my bare love in such a way as to show me worthy of your respect. Then perhaps I may dare to boast how I love you, till then not show my head to prove myself.

Anyone familiar with Elizabethan usage should realise that the phrase, 'lord of my love', l. 1, is to be taken literally as well as figuratively : the young man to whom the Sonnets are addressed is a lord. It has long been realised how closely the language of this sonnet resembles that of Shakespeare's dedication of *Venus and Adonis* to Southampton : 'I know not how I shall offend in dedicating my unpolished lines to your lordship, nor how the world will censure me for choosing so strong a prop to support so weak a burden : only if your Honour seem but pleased, I account myself highly praised, and vow to take advantage of all idle hours till I have honoured you with some graver labour'.

Throughout the sonnet Shakespeare insists on his duty, the service he owes to his patron ; the tone is one of deep respect from the poet towards one of much superior social station. Ll. 9-12 show that Shakespeare was at this time far from prosperous, and hoped for a better turn to his fortunes. The sestet also shows Shakespeare's hope to justify his patron's confidence with the work he intends, with luck, to achieve. These lines convey a tactful hint to a patron. The sonnet reads like a conclusion, an *envoi* to the whole of this first section, Sonnets 1-26, which may well have formed 'this written ambassage to witness duty' to his lord.

27

Weary with toil, I haste me to my bed,
The dear repose for limbs with travel tired ;
But then begins a journey in my head
To work my mind, when body's work's expired.
For then my thoughts, from far where I abide,
Intend a zealous pilgrimage to thee,
And keep my drooping eyelids open wide,
Looking on darkness which the blind do see :
Save that my soul's imaginary sight
Presents thy shadow to my sightless view,
Which, like a jewel hung in ghastly night,
Makes black night beauteous and her old face new.
   Lo, thus, by day my limbs, by night my mind,
   For thee and for myself no quiet find.

27

Weary with toil, I hurry to my bed, the welcome repose for limbs tired out with travel ; but then, when my body's work is over, I begin to journey in mind. For my thoughts make pilgrimage to you, from far away where I am, keeping my eyes wide open into the dark night where only the blind can see: except that my imagination brings your shape before me, hung there like a jewel in the night, making the darkness glow and wear a new face. Thus, my limbs by day, my mind by night, find no rest for either of us.

This sonnet begins a new series, with Shakespeare journeying away from proximity to Southampton, into the country. But he finds a new image for a sonnet to send to his patron — that of the jewel hung in the night. In *Venus and Adonis* contemporaneously we find the word 'shadow' used for 'image', as in l. 10 :

> Narcissus so himself himself forsook,
> And died to kiss his shadow in the brook.

We come to appreciate more clearly that these sonnets are offerings of duty to a patron : we see Shakespeare's invention labouring to give a new turn to the well-worn theme, until a new turn in the personal situation, with its emotional complications, gives fresh inspiration.

The idea that some stones could be seen in the dark is referred to in *Titus Andronicus*, II. iii. 226-30 ; while cf. ll. 11-12 with *Romeo and Juliet*, I. v. 47,

> Her beauty hangs upon the cheek of night
> Like a rich jewel in an Ethiop's ear.

28

How can I then return in happy plight
That am debarred the benefit of rest ?
When day's oppression is not eased by night
But day by night, and night by day, oppressed ?
And each, though enemies to either's reign,
Do in consent shake hands to torture me,
The one by toil, the other to complain
How far I toil, still farther off from thee.
I tell the day to please him thou art bright
And dost him grace when clouds do blot the heaven :
So flatter I the swart-complexioned night
When sparkling stars twire not thou gild'st the even.
    But day doth daily draw my sorrows longer,
    And night doth nightly make grief's strength seem
       stronger.

28

How can I return in good shape, when I am debarred of rest ? When the burdens of the day are not eased by night but I am oppressed by both ? Both combine to wear me out, one by work, the other by complaining that my work carries me still farther away from you. I assure the day that you are bright to please him and shine even when clouds blot out the sun ; I flatter the swarthy night when no star peeps out that you light up the evening. But every day the day draws out my regret, and every night the night makes my grief greater.

We easily perceive that this sonnet was suggested by the previous one and was written as an echo of it. It gives the impression of being a bit jaded : no doubt Shakespeare was tired out, as he complains. However, he manages to make another variation on his theme, even if it sounds artificial. We see in a sonnet like this that such poems were rather offerings of duty. Where was Shakespeare on tour this year ? The next sonnet shows that he had no luck. Only the word 'twire' in l. 12 needs explanation : it means to peep.

29

When, in disgrace with fortune and men's eyes,
I all alone beweep my outcast state,
And trouble deaf heaven with my bootless cries,
And look upon myself, and curse my fate :
Wishing me like to one more rich in hope,
Featured like him, like him with friends possessed,
Desiring this man's art and that man's scope,
With what I most enjoy contented least :
Yet in these thoughts myself almost despising,
Haply I think on thee, and then my state,
Like to the lark at break of day arising
From sullen earth, sings hymns at heaven's gate ;
    For thy sweet love remembered such wealth brings
    That then I scorn to change my state with kings.

29

When down on my luck and with people set against me, all alone I lament my lot as an outsider : but I reproach heaven in vain with my laments, looking upon myself and cursing my fate. I wish myself like one with more hope in life, like him in looks and surrounded with friends ; I find myself envying this man's art and that man's range, least contented with what I most enjoy. In this mood almost despising myself, I happen to think of you : and then, like the lark rising at dawn from sullen earth, I chant hymns to heaven. For thinking of your love brings such wealth to mind that then I would not change my state with kings.

No artificiality in this famous sonnet : the sincerity shines through ; it is extremely revealing, psychologically and autobiographically. But then we remember Ben Jonson's description of Shakespeare as, above all, 'of an open and free nature'. No disguise about him whatever — and perhaps only a man of the people would have given himself away so freely. We learn more from this about Shakespeare's resentment at the circumstances of his life : these years 1592 and 1593 were a period of extreme discouragement, with the closing of the theatres making it difficult to earn a livelihood — a hazardous existence, as Robert Greene, Watson, Kyd, Peele, Marlowe all found, who all came to an end in these years. And in this year 1592 there came, in addition to the disgrace of fortune, the disgrace in 'men's eyes' of Robert Greene's deathbed attack on him in print, which Shakespeare much resented. The reference in l. 8 —

> With what I most enjoy contented least —

would be a reference to his profession as actor. It is not unlikely that, in such moods of depression, he found most dissatisfaction in what gave him most pleasure : his acting. Shakespeare is referring to the fortunate young Earl himself in ll. 5-6.

30

When to the sessions of sweet silent thought
I summon up remembrance of things past,
I sigh the lack of many a thing I sought
And with old woes new wail my dear time's waste :
Then can I drown an eye, unused to flow,
For precious friends hid in death's dateless night,
And weep afresh love's long since cancelled woe,
And moan the expense of many a vanished sight :
Then can I grieve at grievances foregone,
And heavily from woe to woe tell o'er
The sad account of fore-bemoanèd moan,
Which I new pay as if not paid before.
    But if the while I think on thee, dear friend,
    All losses are restored and sorrows end.

30

When in these sessions of silent thought I recall memories of past things, I lament the lack of many a thing I wished for and turn over old sorrows with new regrets : then can I weep, though not much given to tears, for beloved friends now dead ; bewail anew the wounds of former love, regretting what many a vanished sight has cost me. Then can I grieve at past troubles again, and tell over the account of sorrows already lamented, as if I had not paid the score long ago. But if in this mood I think of you, dear friend, all losses are restored and sorrows over.

———

The second line of this sonnet has achieved a world-wide circulation in the literature of the twentieth century, with its concern with time. It was taken for an epigraph by Proust for the greatest of modern novels, *A la Recherche du Temps Perdu*. The mood of depression, with absence from his friend, continues and brings back to Shakespeare the thought of earlier friends now dead, and former loves now over.

Observe the alliteration running all through — second nature to a born poet. L. 5, compare the phrase in *Lucrece*, l. 1239, 'they drown their eyes' ; l. 6, compare *Romeo and Juliet*, V. iii. 115,

A dateless bargain to engrossing death.

31

Thy bosom is endearèd with all hearts,
Which I, by lacking, have supposèd dead ;
And there reigns love, and all love's loving parts,
And all those friends which I thought burièd.
How many a holy and obsequious tear
Hath dear religious love stol'n from mine eye,
As interest of the dead, which now appear
But things removed that hidden in thee lie !
Thou art the grave where buried love doth live,
Hung with the trophies of my lovers gone,
Who all their parts of me to thee did give —
That due of many now is thine alone :
    Their images I loved I view in thee,
    And thou, all they, hast all the all of me.

31

You are the dearer to me for all those whom I have supposed dead ;
for love reigns in your breast, and every part of love, and all those
friends I thought buried. How many a tear has faithful love stolen
from my eye as due to the dead, who now seem to me but absent
and hidden in you ! You are the grave where buried love yet lives,
hung with the trophies of my earlier friends, who gave all their
share in me to you : what belonged to many now is yours alone :
in you I see their loved images, and you, who sum them all up,
have all there is of me.

———

Not an easy sonnet of which to follow the train of thought, based as it
is on a curious conceit, to us today rather far-fetched. It carries on the
thought of the previous sonnet in antiphony : it is a development of it,
obviously written at the same time, perhaps on the same day. The theme
provides something new to offer the young patron. In l. 5 the word
'obsequious' must be given its literal Elizabethan meaning, *i.e.* pertaining
to obsequies.

32

If thou survive my well-contented day
When that churl death my bones with dust shall cover,
And shalt by fortune once more re-survey
These poor rude lines of thy deceasèd lover,
Compare them with the bettering of the time —
And though they be outstripped by every pen,
Reserve them for my love, not for their rhyme,
Exceeded by the height of happier men.
O, then vouchsafe me but this loving thought :
'Had my friend's Muse grown with this growing age,
A dearer birth than this his love had brought,
To march in ranks of better equipage :
   But since he died, and poets better prove,
   Theirs for their style I'll read, his for his love.'

———————

This little-known and never-quoted sonnet yet tells us much. Underneath the inverted commas, so to speak, there is a charming modesty. Shakespeare sees the age as one of improvement in the art of verse, and it was just in these years that the sonnet-vogue got going with the publication of Sidney's *Astrophil and Stella* in 1591, Daniel's *Delia*, and Constable's *Diana* in 1592, Drayton's *Idea* in 1593, etc. Shakespeare's Sonnets, however, were unlike anyone else's : in the fact that they were addressed to a man, for one thing, in their reality and power, in the openness and intimacy of their confession, their autobiographical content and the equivocal, tortured story they proceed to reveal : all this made for their unsuitability for publication, unlike the other literary sonnet-sequences.

Underneath the self-deprecation one must not miss, with such a clever man, an element of irony. He knew his own worth.

32

If you survive my accepted span, when death has covered my bones with dust, and by chance read over these poor lines of your dead friend, comparing them with the progress of the age — though they may be outstripped by every pen, keep them for my love, not for their verse, exceeded by the attainments of those more fortunate. Grant me then but this loving thought : 'had my friend's muse grown with this improving age, he would have achieved a better offspring than this, to march in better appointed ranks. But since he died, and poets write better now, I'll read them for their style, him for his love.'

With the Elizabethans, with their more poetic ways of expression, the word 'lover' was sometimes used where we should use 'friend'. The Augustan Malone sagely lays down, 'such addresses to men were common in Shakespeare's time, and were not thought indecorous'. In fact it was a recognised expression, rather than a common one, more in place in verse.

In l. 7, 'reserve them for my love', it is nice to think that this is just what happened : at any rate, they were reserved, *i.e.* kept, and so we have them.

This concludes the section, Sonnets 27-32, which go together and were evidently written in absence ; this is a kind of dedication and they may have been sent together.

33

Full many a glorious morning have I seen
Flatter the mountain-tops with sovereign eye,
Kissing with golden face the meadows green,
Gilding pale streams with heavenly alchemy,
Anon permit the basest clouds to ride
With ugly rack on his celestial face,
And from the forlorn world his visage hide,
Stealing unseen to west with this disgrace.
Even so my sun one early morn did shine
With all-triumphant splendour on my brow ;
But out, alack ! he was but one hour mine,
The region cloud hath masked him from me now.
    Yet him for this my love no whit disdaineth ;
    Suns of the world may stain when heaven's sun staineth.

33

Often have I seen a glorious morning light up the hills, bathe the green meadows in golden sunshine, changing the colour of the streams ; and then lowering clouds drive across the sun's face, hiding it from the world, overcast while the sun steals on to the west unseen. Even so my sun one morning shone with splendour on me ; but then, alas, this was but for an hour : a cloud masks him from me now. Yet love thinks no less of him for this ; when the sun in heaven may be overcast, so may the suns in the world beneath.

———

This sonnet announces the first cloud over the friendship, gently enough. The Elizabethans often called the hills of the West Country or the Pennines, mountains. We need not go further than the Cotswolds for the mountain-tops that Shakespeare had often seen touched with the morning sun : they extend a sickle-shaped high ridge to the south and west of Stratford, beyond the meadows and streams that also figure in the picture. This cloud, like everything else, Shakespeare puts to good use for his patron's amusement. Ll. 1-4 have a close parallel in *Venus and Adonis*, ll. 856-8.

34

Why didst thou promise such a beauteous day
And make me travel forth without my cloak,
To let base clouds o'ertake me in my way,
Hiding thy bravery in their rotten smoke ?
'Tis not enough that through the cloud thou break,
To dry the rain on my storm-beaten face,
For no man well of such a salve can speak
That heals the wound and cures not the disgrace :
Nor can thy shame give physic to my grief —
Though thou repent, yet I have still the loss :
The offender's sorrow lends but weak relief
To him that bears the strong offence's cross.
   Ah, but those tears are pearl which thy love sheds,
   And they are rich and ransom all ill deeds.

34

Why did you promise that all was well, so that I took no precaution, and have been caught by this cloud upon our friendship, darkening your transparent candour with suspicion? It's not enough that you should break through the cloud to dry my tears and console me, for no one can think well of a repentance that heals the wound but does not remove the cause of it. Nor can your shame console my grief — though you repent, I still suffer the consequences : the offender's regret affords little relief to him that bears the heavy cross of the offence. And yet — those tears are pearls when you shed them in love : they richly ransom all ill deeds.

With this we enter upon the serious story of the Sonnets, with their complexities of feeling, their anguish of mind, the depths of experience they plumb. For what has happened, as we shall see, is that the young man who is so reluctant to marry has taken, or been captured by, Shakespeare's mistress — the dark woman of the later sonnets. These are not later in time : it becomes clear that the story as it unfolds from Sonnets 33 and 34 is duplicated and viewed from the point of view of Shakespeare's relationship to his mistress precisely one hundred sonnets later in the numbering, *i.e.* from 133 onwards. From their place in the sequence this breach of faith would seem to have taken place in Shakespeare's absence. In this situation one cannot but be struck by the dignity, the independence with which Shakespeare speaks out to his lordly young patron. The youth repents in tears and assurance of friendship : it is that that persuades Shakespeare to forgive him.

35

No more be grieved at that which thou hast done :
Roses have thorns, and silver fountains mud ;
Clouds and eclipses stain both moon and sun,
And loathsome canker lives in sweetest bud.
All men make faults, and even I in this,
Authorising thy trespass with compare,
Myself corrupting, salving thy amiss,
Excusing thy sins more than thy sins are :
For to thy sensual fault I bring in sense —
Thy adverse party is thy advocate —
And 'gainst myself a lawful plea commence :
Such civil war is in my love and hate,
    That I an accessory needs must be
    To that sweet thief which sourly robs from me.

35

Do not grieve any more at what you have done : roses have thorns, and clear fountains mud. Clouds and eclipses darken both sun and moon, and in the sweetest bud there may be canker. Everybody commits faults, and even I in this, justifying your fault by producing parallels, myself corrupting you by condoning your misdeed, finding more excuse for you than I find offence. For I bring in reason on the side of your sensual fault — your opponent in the case is your advocate — and start a lawful plea against myself : I am so torn in two between love and resentment that I must be an accessory to the loved thief that robs me.

The conceit that runs through this sonnet is that of a case at law — a natural enough train of thought in the circumstances, though no action would lie. On the psychological plane we observe Shakespeare's sweetness of nature, his readiness to forgive and take blame to himself. Nevertheless, such is the duplicity of things, we must remember that Shakespeare is also partly dependent upon the young man. The situation, between a gentlemanly actor-poet and a spoiled young peer, is not the less surprising. It is like nothing else in our literature. Ll. 6-8 may be a little difficult for the reader, yet their meaning is quite clear.

36

Let me confess that we two must be twain,
Although our undivided loves are one :
So shall those blots that do with me remain,
Without thy help, by me be borne alone.
In our two loves there is but one respect,
Though in our lives a separable spite,
Which though it alters not love's sole effect,
Yet doth it steal sweet hours from love's delight.
I may not evermore acknowledge thee,
Lest my bewailèd guilt should do thee shame,
Nor thou with public kindness honour me,
Unless thou take that honour from thy name.
  But do not so : I love thee in such sort
  As, thou being mine, mine is thy good report.

36

I confess that we are divided, though in love we are one ; so may
those disadvantages I suffer from, without your aid, be borne by me
alone. In our loves there is the same regard for each other, though
the circumstances of our lives must keep us apart ; and though that
does not alter the feeling we have for each other, it does take away
time from delight in each other's company. I may not always show
that I know you in public, lest my own guilt should bring shame on
you ; nor you honour me with open kindness, lest this detracts from
the honour of your name. Do not risk this : my feeling for you is
such that, since you are mine, your good name is my chief care.

———

With some breach of trust between them an explanation is necessary :
here it is, and it is very revealing. Shakespeare recognises the world of
difference there is between their stations, and in the phrase, 'without thy
help', l. 4, we may infer that, dependent as he is on Southampton's help
in the discouraging circumstances of his life, he is prepared to shoulder
them alone. But now, too, Shakespeare has to acknowledge his guilty
relations with his mistress, which are publicly known, for he does not wish
to besmirch his patron's good name by recognising him, or being recognised, in public. An element of surreptitiousness has entered into their
relations : the snake in what was paradise at the beginning.

37

As a decrepit father takes delight
To see his active child do deeds of youth,
So I, made lame by fortune's dearest spite,
Take all my comfort of thy worth and truth ;
For whether beauty, birth, or wealth, or wit,
Or any of these all, or all, or more,
Entitled in thy parts do crownèd sit,
I make my love engrafted to this store :
So then I am not lame, poor, nor despised
Whilst that this shadow doth such substance give
That I in thy abundance am sufficed
And by a part of all thy glory live.
    Look, what is best, that best I wish in thee :
    This wish I have ; then ten times happy me !

37

As a decrepit father takes delight in seeing his child active and youthful, so I, hampered by ill fortune, derive all my comfort from your goodness and true heart. Whether beauty or birth, wealth or wit, stand out royally among your noble gifts, I add my love to the store. Then I no longer feel unfortunate, poor and despised, while this protection gives me such strength that in your abundance I am content, and live as a part of your glory. Whatever is best, that I wish in and for you : this wish I have, and in that am ten times blessed.

———

After the explanation of the previous sonnet, it is natural that there should be an emotional let-up, and this sonnet describes a more relaxed mood. There is also a slightly parental note struck at the beginning, which we have observed before. Notice l. 7 :

Entitled in thy parts do crownèd sit :

those familiar with the ways of Elizabethan writing will recognise the oblique reference to the fact that the friend bore a title. The sonnet provides yet another expression of Shakespeare's resentment at his station, his ill-fortune in not being independent, his set-backs, slights endured, etc. The theme runs all through the Sonnets.

38

How can my Muse want subject to invent
While thou dost breathe, that pour'st into my verse
Thine own sweet argument, too excellent
For every vulgar paper to rehearse ?
O, give thyself the thanks, if aught in me
Worthy perusal stand against thy sight ;
For who's so dumb that cannot write to thee,
When thou thyself dost give invention light ?
Be thou the tenth Muse, ten times more in worth
Than those old nine which rhymers invocate ;
And he that calls on thee, let him bring forth
Eternal numbers to outlive long date.
   If my slight Muse do please these curious days,
   The pain be mine, but thine shall be the praise.

38

How can my verse want a subject while you breathe and give me a theme too excellent for vulgar pens ? Give yourself the thanks if anything I have written is worthy your reading ; for who is so dumb as not to be able to write when you inspire ? Let you become the tenth Muse, worth ten times more than the old nine whom poets invoke ; and let him that invokes you bring forth verse that will live for ever. If my slight Muse please this fastidious age, let the effort be mine and yours the praise.

The relaxed mood continues, but the poem has several points of interest. It serves to reinforce the view that the Sonnets were written as a regular part of the poet's service to his patron. It is interesting to have Shakespeare's view of his age as 'curious', which meant then fastidious, seeking for novelties. It is not an approving judgment ; himself was traditional and conservative.

39

O, how thy worth with manners may I sing,
When thou art all the better part of me ?
What can mine own praise to mine own self bring ?
And what is't but mine own when I praise thee ?
Even for this let us divided live,
And our dear love lose name of single one,
That by this separation I may give
That due to thee which thou deserv'st alone.
O absence, what a torment wouldst thou prove
Were it not thy sour leisure gave sweet leave
To entertain the time with thoughts of love,
Which time and thoughts so sweetly doth deceive,
   And that thou teachest how to make one twain
   By praising him here who doth hence remain.

39

How can I with modesty praise your worth, when you are the better part of me ? What can my own praises award myself, and what is it but my own when I praise you ? Let us live divided, then, and our love forego its singleness, that by this separation I may give you that due which you deserve alone. What a torment absence would be did it not give leisure to occupy the time with thoughts of love, beguiling both time and thoughts, and if it did not teach how to make one into two by praising him here who in fact is absent.

———

In this Shakespeare contrives yet another ingenious variation, evidently written in absence. It is Southampton who is absent now ; once more Shakespeare accepts their inevitable separateness. L. 11 has become so familiar as to be almost proverbial ; it has a parallel in *Lucrece*, l. 1361 :

The weary time she cannot entertain.

40

Take all my loves, my love, yea, take them all :
What hast thou then more than thou hadst before ?
No love, my love, that thou mayst true love call ;
All mine was thine before thou hadst this more.
Then, if for my love thou my love receivest,
I cannot blame thee for my love thou usest ;
But yet be blamed, if thou this self deceivest
By wilful taste of what thyself refusest.
I do forgive thy robbery, gentle thief,
Although thou steal thee all my poverty ;
And yet, love knows, it is a greater grief
To bear love's wrong than hate's known injury.
    Lascivious grace, in whom all ill well shows,
    Kill me with spites, yet we must not be foes.

40

Take all my loves, take them all : what have you got more than you
had before ? Nothing, my dearest, that may be called true love ;
all mine was yours before you had this in addition.. Then, if you
take to yourself my lover out of love for me, I cannot blame you
for using her ; and yet you may be blamed, if you deceive me by
wilfully tasting what you refuse in lawful union. I forgive your
robbery, though you steal all I have ; yet, love knows it is harder
to bear the wrong love does than the injury of hate. Lascivious grace,
in whom even ill shows attractive, injure me as you will, so long
as we do not become enemies.

This important sonnet offers some difficulty, the situation is so equivocal
beneath the polite language of conceit. The young patron has taken his
poet's mistress — though Shakespeare does not call that relation 'true
love'. Shakespeare does not reproach him for taking her, but for taking
her while himself refusing to marry. There is an implied reproach, too, in
the young lord taking from his poet's poverty. But what are we to make
of l. 5 ? —

Then, if for my love thou my love receivest.

Southampton became acquainted with the lady through writing to her on
Shakespeare's behalf. But what could Shakespeare have done about it,
in his situation of poverty and dependence ? He evidently decided to
make the best of it. Not very dignified ; but, then, he was not in a
position to stand on his dignity.

41

Those pretty wrongs that liberty commits,
When I am sometime absent from thy heart,
Thy beauty and thy years full well befits,
For still temptation follows where thou art.
Gentle thou art, and therefore to be won,
Beauteous thou art, therefore to be assailed.
And when a woman woos, what woman's son
Will sourly leave her till she have prevailed?
Ay me! but yet thou mightst my seat forbear,
And chide thy beauty and thy straying youth,
Who lead thee in their riot even there
Where thou art forced to break a twofold truth:
  Hers, by thy beauty tempting her to thee,
  Thine, by thy beauty being false to me.

41

Those engaging wrongs you commit, when I am sometimes absent from your heart, befit your youth and beauty, for temptation follows you wherever you are. You are gentle, and therefore to be won ; handsome, and therefore to be tried. And when a woman woos, what woman's son will leave her till she has had her way ? Yet, alas, you might forbear to take my place, and restrain your erring youth that leads you to where you are forced to make a double breach of faith : hers, tempted by your good looks ; yours, in being false to me.

———

This sonnet, after the covert language of the preceding one, makes the situation quite explicit : the poet's mistress is after the young peer, and he is willing. Shakespeare needed all his tact to support it, and tact of expression to express it. The reproach is expressed in terms of praise. Needs must ; but the subtlety lies in that it is also genuine.

Ll. 7-8 : notice the closeness to *Venus and Adonis*, ll. 201-2 :

> Art thou a woman's son and canst not feel
> What 'tis to love, how want of love tormenteth ?

42

That thou hast her it is not all my grief,
And yet it may be said I loved her dearly ;
That she hath thee is of my wailing chief,
A loss in love that touches me more nearly.
Loving offenders, thus I will excuse ye :
Thou dost love her, because thou know'st I love her ;
And for my sake even so doth she abuse me,
Suffering my friend for my sake to approve her.
If I lose thee, my loss is my love's gain,
And losing her, my friend hath found that loss :
Both find each other, and I lose both twain,
And both for my sake lay on me this cross.
   But here's the joy : my friend and I are one ;
   Sweet flattery ! then she loves but me alone.

42

It is not my main ground of complaint that you have her, even though I loved her dearly ; that she has you is my chief regret, a loss that touches me more closely. Loving offenders, I excuse you thus : you love her, because you know I love her ; similarly she abuses me for my sake, in allowing my friend to try her. If I lose you, my loss is a gain to my love ; and losing her, my friend picks up the loss. Both find each other, I lose both, and both lay this cross on me for my sake. But there is consolation in this thought : my friend and I are one, therefore she loves but me alone.

———

It says something for the resources of poetry, and the resilience of the poet, to be able to go on making variations in this complication of the theme. Shakespeare has to content himself with a poor consolation at the end, but 'beggars can't be choosers'. The sonnet is an *envoi* to the section 33-42. The subject of the imbroglio, the triangular relationship, is taken up more fully and treated more seriously in the Dark Lady sequence, Sonnet 127 foll., from the different angle of Shakespeare's relations with her.

43

When most I wink then do mine eyes best see,
For all the day they view things unrespected ;
But when I sleep, in dreams they look on thee,
And, darkly bright, are bright in dark directed.
And thou, whose shadow shadows doth make bright,
How would thy shadow's form form happy show
To the clear day with thy much clearer light,
When to unseeing eyes thy shade shines so !
How would, I say, mine eyes be blessèd made
By looking on thee in the living day,
When in dead night thy fair imperfect shade
Through heavy sleep on sightless eyes doth stay !
    All days are nights to see till I see thee,
    And nights bright days when dreams do show thee me.

43

When most I close my eyes then do I see best, for all day I look at things unconsidered ; but sleeping I see you in dreams : my eyes, darkly bright, are clearly directed in the dark. And you, whose image makes darkness bright, how would your form itself show happy in clear daylight when to closed eyes your shade shines so ! How blessed should I be to look on you in the living day, when in the dead of night your shadow is imprinted on closed eyes in sleep ! All days are like dark nights till I see you, and nights like bright days when dreams reveal you to me.

―――――

This sonnet starts a new series written in absence. That this is written in duty is obvious. Shakespeare is repeating himself, cf. Sonnet 27.

44

If the dull substance of my flesh were thought,
Injurious distance should not stop my way ;
For then, despite of space, I would be brought,
From limits far remote where thou dost stay.
No matter then although my foot did stand
Upon the farthest earth removed from thee ;
For nimble thought can jump both sea and land,
As soon as think the place where he would be.
But, ah ! thought kills me that I am not thought,
To leap large lengths of miles when thou art gone,
But that, so much of earth and water wrought,
I must attend time's leisure with my moan ;
    Receiving nought by elements so slow
    But heavy tears, badges of either's woe.

44

If only the heavy substance of my body were turned into thought, the disadvantage of distance would not hold me up ; for then, in spite of space, I should be brought from far away to where you are. It would not matter whether I were at the farthest limit of earth from you, for swift thought can jump sea and land as soon as think where one would be. Alas, it kills me to think that I am not thought, to leap over the long miles between us, but that, being made so much of the heavier elements, I must await time's leisure, receiving from these nothing but heavy tears, emblems of each other's grief.

———

The thought of this sonnet is not altogether easy ; the idea it plays with is that of the two heavy elements, earth and water, according to Elizabethan science ; the two light elements being air and fire. Of these was the universe supposed to be composed. The situation is that Southampton is absent.

45

The other two, slight air and purging fire,
Are both with thee, wherever I abide :
The first my thought, the other my desire,
These present-absent with swift motion slide.
For when these quicker elements are gone
In tender embassy of love to thee,
My life, being made of four, with two alone
Sinks down to death, oppressed with melancholy.
Until life's composition be recured
By those swift messengers returned from thee,
Who even but now come back again, assured
Of thy fair health, recounting it to me :
   This told, I joy ; but then no longer glad,
   I send them back again, and straight grow sad.

45

The other two elements, air and fire, are with you, wherever I am :
the first is my thought, the second my desire, these swiftly inter-
changing presence with absence. When these lighter elements are
gone on embassy to you, my life, being made of four, sinks down
to heaviness and melancholy. Until the proper composition of
life is recovered by those swift messengers returned from you, who
even at this moment come back, assuring me of your good health.
Hearing this, I am happy ; and then, sending back thought and
desire to you again, I am left sad.

This continues and completes the thought of Sonnet 44 : the two go
together, composed together in absence, as offerings of duty. We notice
how often the sonnets go in pairs, the thought or conceit of one being
complemented or returned in a second, as if antiphonally. A good way
of spinning out poems to meet requirements.

46

Mine eye and heart are at a mortal war
How to divide the conquest of thy sight :
Mine eye, my heart thy picture's sight would bar,
My heart, mine eye the freedom of that right.
My heart doth plead that thou in him dost lie —
A closet never pierced with crystal eyes —
But the defendant doth that plea deny,
And says in him thy fair appearance lies.
To 'cide this title is impanellèd
A quest of thoughts, all tenants to the heart,
And by their verdict is determinèd
The clear eye's moiety and the dear heart's part :
   As thus : mine eye's due is thine outward part,
   And my heart's right thine inward love of heart.

46

My eye and heart are in conflict how to divide the conquest of your image. The eye would debar the heart of the sight of your picture, the heart deny the eye any such right. The heart pleads that you lie there — a closet never pierced by mortal eyes ; but the defendant denies this and claims that your appearance lies in him. To decide this a jury of thoughts is impanelled — all of them the heart's tenants — and their verdict determines the issue between eye and heart. In this wise : your outward part is the eye's due, your inner heart's love is my heart's right.

———

Never was there more obviously a duty-sonnet : all too ingenious and unmoving to our taste. However, Elizabethan taste was another matter. Contemporary life is reflected in the image of impanelling the jury, the tenants of the manor : their verdict was to award a 'moiety', l. 12, *i.e.* one-half, to each. We still retain the word 'quest' in local country speech : a 'crowner's quest' means coroner's inquest.

47

Betwixt mine eye and heart a league is took,
And each doth good turns now unto the other :
When that mine eye is famished for a look,
Or heart in love with sighs himself doth smother,
With my love's picture then my eye doth feast,
And to the painted banquet bids my heart ;
Another time mine eye is my heart's guest
And in his thoughts of love doth share a part.
So, either by thy picture or my love,
Thyself away art present still with me ;
For thou not farther than my thoughts canst move,
And I am still with them and they with thee.
   Or, if they sleep, thy picture in my sight
   Awakes my heart to heart's and eye's delight.

47

A league is made between eye and heart, and now each does good turns to the other : when my eye is famished for a look or my heart smothered in sighs, the one feasts on my love's picture and bids the heart to that painted feast ; another time the eye is the heart's guest and shares in its thoughts of love. So, either by your picture or my love, you are still present with me when away ; for you are not farther than my thoughts can move, and I am with them as they are with you. Or, if they are asleep, your picture in my sight awakes both eye and heart to pleasure.

————

This continues.the thought of the previous poem, and is its antiphon, or chime. We may infer from it that Southampton had given his poet a picture of himself — perhaps a miniature, which Shakespeare carried with him in his absence. L. 3 is closely paralleled in *The Comedy of Errors*, II. i. 88 :

Whilst I at home starve for a merry look.

48

How careful was I, when I took my way,
Each trifle under truest bars to thrust,
That to my use it might unusèd stay
From hands of falsehood, in sure wards of trust !
But thou, to whom my jewels trifles are,
Most worthy comfort, now my greatest grief,
Thou best of dearest and mine only care,
Art left the prey of every vulgar thief.
Thee have I not locked up in any chest,
Save where thou art not, though I feel thou art,
Within the gentle closure of my breast,
From whence at pleasure thou mayst come and part ;
   And even thence thou wilt be stol'n, I fear,
   For truth proves thievish for a prize so dear.

48

How careful I was, when I went away, to put every trifle under lock
and key that it might remain shut up safely, untouched by thievish
hands. But you, to whom my trinkets are but trifles — my dearest
comfort and now my chief concern, my fondest love and only care
— are left the prey of every common thief. I have not been able to
lock you up in any chest, save where you are not — though I feel
you are — within my breast, whence you may come and go as you
will. And I fear you will be stolen even from there, for honesty
itself turns thief for so dear a prize.

———————

Suggestive autobiographically ; we see Shakespeare, on leaving his room
in London, locking up his few possessions. But he cannot put the young
Earl under lock and key : he remains there, a prey to any who attempt
him. We hear the accents of apprehension and mistrust, for the young
man, during Shakespeare's absence, is the object of his mistress's atten-
tions. The latter receives a kind, if oblique, compliment in the last line,
'for truth proves thievish' : we shall see how true she was. On the
other hand, there is Shakespeare's intense and intimate concern for Southampton : 'thou best of dearest and mine only care'. (What about the
family at Stratford ? Well, Shakespeare was doing his best to maintain
them. His relation to his patron was part of that too.) How complex
it has all become, in the manner of such things, after the simplicity of the
beginning ! Again we note a certain protective, quasi-parental feeling
on the part of the poet.
    L. 4 : we still use the word 'wards', though rarely : it means the
notches on key and lock that fit each other.

49

Against that time, if ever that time come,
When I shall see thee frown on my defects,
When as thy love hath cast his utmost sum,
Called to that audit by advised respects :
Against that time when thou shalt strangely pass,
And scarcely greet me with that sun, thine eye,
When love, converted from the thing it was,
Shall reasons find of settled gravity :
Against that time do I ensconce me here
Within the knowledge of mine own desert,
And this my hand against myself uprear,
To guard the lawful reasons on thy part :
   To leave poor me thou hast the strength of laws,
   Since why to love I can allege no cause.

49

Against the time, if ever it comes, when I shall see you frown on my failings, when your love closes its account, arrived at on careful consideration of circumstances : against the time when you will pass me like a stranger, scarcely seeing me, when love has ceased to be what it was and has to find good reasons : against that time I fortify myself in the knowledge of what I deserve, and raise my own hand against myself to witness your right to disown me. You have every right to leave poor me, since there is no reason why you should love me.

There is no mistaking the accents of sincerity in this fine sonnet. Sadness chimes throughout it in the thrice repeated 'against that time' ; but there is also the psychological prevision of the inevitable, and — what is so characteristic of Shakespeare — the acceptance. There is no illusion about the relationship between the proud young peer and the poor poet whom he is pleased to favour, between the handsome youth and the older man, who accepts the inevitability of 'that time when thou shalt strangely pass and scarcely greet me'. No doubt it came. Years later, in *Julius Caesar*, IV. ii. 21, there is a reflection of this :

> When love begins to sicken and decay,
> It useth an enforcèd ceremony.

At the same time, the figures used are those of an account, the last sum in the audit, raising one's hand in a court of law as witness, being left poor. There is the reminder, so tactfully put, of the poet's dependence on his patron : reverse 'poor me', in l. 13, to read 'to leave me poor', and one gets the hint.

Observe, in this awkward situation, Shakespeare's characteristic grand language, the tactful abstractness of 'advised respects', 'reasons find of settled gravity'.

50

How heavy do I journey on the way
When what I seek, my weary travel's end,
Doth teach that ease and that repose to say,
'Thus far the miles are measured from thy friend.'
The beast that bears me, tired with my woe,
Plods dully on, to bear that weight in me,
As if by some instinct the wretch did know
His rider loved not speed, being made from thee :
The bloody spur cannot provoke him on
That sometimes anger thrusts into his hide,
Which heavily he answers with a groan,
More sharp to me than spurring to his side ;
    For that same groan doth put this in my mind :
    My grief lies onward, and my joy behind.

50

How heavily I jog on my way, when what I seek — my weary journey's end — speaks to me, when I reach my repose, only of the miles that I have measured away from my friend. The poor beast that bears me — sick at heart — plods dully on, as if by some instinct he knows that his rider does not want speed, since it takes him away from you. Even the spur does not drive him on, when sometimes impatiently I thrust it into his side : he answers with a groan that pierces me more than the spur does him — for it puts me in mind that my grief lies before me, my happiness behind.

———

After the psychological complexity of the previous sonnet, we are grateful for the simplicity of this : a picture of Shakespeare journeying on his horse into the country, away from London and his patron, probably on tour, or perhaps going home to Stratford.

51

Thus can my love excuse the slow offence
Of my dull bearer, when from thee I speed :
From where thou art, why should I haste me thence ?
Till I return, of posting is no need.
O, what excuse will my poor beast then find,
When swift extremity can seem but slow ?
Then should I spur, though mounted on the wind,
In wingèd speed no motion shall I know :
Then can no horse with my desire keep pace.
Therefore desire, of perfect'st love being made,
Shall neigh, no dull flesh, in his fiery race ;
But love, for love, thus shall excuse my jade :
   Since from thee going he went wilful-slow,
   Towards thee I'll run and give him leave to go.

51

Thus can my love excuse the slowness of my horse in going from you : from where you are, why should I haste away ? Until I return, there is no need of hurrying. But what excuse will my poor beast find then, when the fastest speed will seem slow to me ? Then I should spur, if I were mounted on the wind, nor even feel any motion however swift : no horse could keep pace with my desire. Therefore desire, being made of the most perfect love, shall cry out — no mere flesh — in a fiery race. Love, in return for love, shall excuse my steed : since going away from you he went wilfully slow, in returning I shall race and let him walk.

———

The companion-piece to Sonnet 50, rather laboured to our taste. A duty-piece, though the feeling is genuine enough : it is a little difficult to follow the thought of ll. 11-12. It is more pleasing to reflect that Shakespeare was a good judge of horse-flesh, and had a fellow-feeling for his poor beast of burden.

52

So am I as the rich, whose blessèd key
Can bring him to his sweet up-lockèd treasure,
The which he will not every hour survey,
For blunting the fine point of seldom pleasure.
Therefore are feasts so solemn and so rare
Since, seldom coming, in the long year set,
Like stones of worth they thinly placèd are,
Or captain jewels in the carcanet.
So is the time that keeps you as my chest,
Or as the wardrobe which the robe doth hide,
To make some special instant special blest,
By new unfolding his imprisoned pride.
    Blessèd are you, whose worthiness gives scope,
      Being had — to triumph, being lacked — to hope.

52

Thus am I like a rich man, whose key can open to him his locked-up treasure, which he is not for ever looking at, lest he should lose the exquisite pleasure by enjoying it too often. Therefore are feasts so rare and cherished, since, coming seldom in the year, they are spaced out like the finest jewels in a necklace. So time operates that keeps you as my chest, or as a wardrobe concealing the robe, to make some special moment specially blessed, unfolding it to reveal the sight of you withheld from me. Thus are you blessed, whose worth has such power that in your presence I triumph, in absence I hope for your return.

———

How ingenious ! this reminds us again how clever a writer, apart from anything else, Shakespeare was ; with what ease he wrote these endless variations on his theme. This goes back to the theme of Sonnet 48, of the poet's locked chest with its few possessions, and the key. There is the extraordinary ease and conciseness of such a line as l. 4, impossible to render as pointedly in prose. It is clear that Shakespeare saw his patron only at intervals.

53

What is your substance, whereof are you made,
That millions of strange shadows on you tend ?
Since every one hath, every one, one shade,
And you, but one, can every shadow lend.
Describe Adonis, and the counterfeit
Is poorly imitated after you ;
On Helen's cheek all art of beauty set,
And you in Grecian tires are painted new :
Speak of the spring and foison of the year,
The one doth shadow of your beauty show,
The other as your bounty doth appear ;
And you in every blessèd shape we know.
 In all external grace you have some part,
 But you like none, none you, for constant heart.

53

Of what substance are you made, that innumerable shadows attend on you ? Everyone has but one shadow, yet you — only one person — can cast every shadow. Describe Adonis, and the description is a poor imitation of you ; set out Helen in all her beauty, and you appear anew in Grecian guise. Speak of spring and harvest : the one is the shadow of your beauty, as the other is of your bounty : we recognise you in every good shape we know. In all external graces you have some share, but there is none like you for constancy of heart.

———

From the relaxed ease of this, the sense of gratitude, the emphasis on Southampton's generosity of heart, I think we may infer that the poet had been the recipient of his patron's bounty. There is less anxiety in these sonnets. At this time Adonis, ll. 5-6, was much in mind, for Shakespeare was writing *Venus and Adonis* for his young patron, describing him in it recognisably as Adonis. The comparison with Helen reminds us of Sonnet 20 and the description of Southampton as combining the best of both masculine and feminine attractions. This was very much a Renaissance theme, as in the court-poems addressed to Henri III.

54

O, how much more doth beauty beauteous seem
By that sweet ornament which truth doth give !
The rose looks fair, but fairer we it deem
For that sweet odour which doth in it live.
The canker-blooms have full as deep a dye
As the perfumèd tincture of the roses,
Hang on such thorns, and play as wantonly
When summer's breath their maskèd buds discloses :
But, for their virtue only is their show,
They live unwooed and unrespected fade,
Die to themselves.   Sweet roses do not so :
Of their sweet deaths are sweetest odours made :
   And so of you, beauteous and lovely youth,
   When that shall fade, by verse distils your truth.

54

How much more admirable is beauty when the quality of truth is added to it ! The rose looks fair, but we think more highly of it for the fragrance it has. Scentless wild roses have as good a colour as the scented rose, flower on such thorns, and play as prettily in the summer breeze that opens their buds. But their only merit is their show : we do not pluck them and they fade unregarded, die on their own. With scented roses it is not so : they perish to create sweet essences. And so of you, lovely youth, when that fades, verse will distil your quality.

———

In the sonnets of this section one has the impression of anxiety relaxed, a sense of gratitude : which Shakespeare repays by promising his patron immortality in his verse. The promise was fulfilled. L. 12, 'Of their sweet deaths are sweetest odours made' : it is touching to hear the echo of this, years later, towards the end of Shakespeare's life, in *The Tempest* : 'Of his bones are coral made'.

55

Not marble, nor the gilded monuments
Of princes, shall outlive this powerful rhyme ;
But you shall shine more bright in these contents
Than unswept stone, besmeared with sluttish time.
When wasteful war shall statues overturn,
And broils root out the work of masonry,
Nor Mars's sword nor war's quick fire shall burn
The living record of your memory.
'Gainst death and all-oblivious enmity
Shall you pace forth : your praise shall still find room
Even in the eyes of all posterity
That wear this world out to the ending doom.
    So, till the judgment that yourself arise,
    You live in this, and dwell in lovers' eyes.

55

Neither marble nor princes' gilded monuments shall outlive these verses : you shall shine more bright in them than unswept stone, dirty with decay. When war shall overturn statues and throw down buildings, neither sword nor fire shall destroy the living record of your memory. Against death and injurious oblivion shall you go forward : your praise shall still find place even in the eyes of posterity, until doomsday ends the world. So, till the day of judgment calls you to arise, you will live on in this and in the eyes of lovers.

———

All that one can say about this famous sonnet, this splendid incantation, is to notice the outburst of confidence in his verse on the part of the poet, hitherto so modest. Perhaps it came, naturally enough, along with the relief of his anxiety. Nor was he wrong : wars have come and gone, London been twice burnt down, yet Shakespeare's friend goes on immortally in his verse, as the poet assured him.

56

Sweet love, renew thy force : be it not said
Thy edge should blunter be than appetite,
Which but today by feeding is allayed,
Tomorrow sharpened in his former might.
So, love, be thou : although today thou fill
Thy hungry eyes even till they wink with fulness,
Tomorrow see again, and do not kill
The spirit of love with a perpetual dulness.
Let this sad interim like the ocean be
Which parts the shore, where two contracted new
Come daily to the banks, that when they see
Return of love, more blest may be the view.
   Or call it winter, which, being full of care,
   Makes summer's welcome thrice more wished, more
      rare.

56

Love, renew your power : let it not be weaker than desire, which today is satisfied but tomorrow is revived. So, love, with you : although today you fill your hungry eyes to the full, tomorrow open them wide again : do not allow the spirit of love to sink into drowsiness. Let this sad interval be like the sea parting the shore, where two betrothed lovers come daily to the sea-side, to see a view made happier by the return of love. Or like winter, which, being full of care, makes the arrival of summer all the more rare and desirable.

It is a little difficult to be sure of the situation here : there is a certain feeling of drifting apart in the poem. What does 'sad interim', l. 9, imply? I do not think it is merely absence. The poet would seem to be whipping up the young man's flagging affection. Behind ll. 9-12 flickers a reminiscence of the situation of Hero and Leander.

57

Being your slave, what should I do but tend
Upon the hours and times of your desire?
I have no precious time at all to spend,
Nor services to do, till you require.
Nor dare I chide the world-without-end hour
Whilst I, my sovereign, watch the clock for you,
Nor think the bitterness of absence sour
When you have bid your servant once adieu.
Nor dare I question with my jealous thought
Where you may be, or your affairs suppose,
But like a sad slave stay and think of nought
Save, where you are, how happy you make those.
 So true a fool is love that in your will,
 Though you do anything, he thinks no ill.

57

Being your slave, what should I do but wait upon the timing of
your wishes ? I have nothing to do with my time, no services to
perform, till you command. Nor do I complain of the tedious
hours while I watch the clock for you, nor think absence bitter
when you have bidden your servant adieu. Nor dare I question
jealously where you may be, or what you may be doing, but sadly
wait and think of nothing but that, with whomever you may be,
you make them happy. So devoted a fool is love that whatever
you wish or do, he thinks no ill.

I fear this takes us into the reality of the situation. One sees the picture :
the spoiled young peer, with his lordly ways, keeping the older man, his
poet and servant, waiting on his pleasure. One sees Shakespeare kept
waiting, while his lord is elsewhere, out and about. Shakespeare's time
does not matter ; it is his to wait on his young master. Underneath the
sad dignity of the polite phrasing, one recognises the accents of reproach
and of a gentle irony. L. 13 has a play on the word 'will', emphasised in
the original with a capital, 'Will', for Shakespeare himself.

58

That God forbid, that made me first your slave,
I should in thought control your times of pleasure,
Or at your hand the account of hours to crave,
Being your vassal, bound to stay your leisure.
O let me suffer, being at your beck,
The imprisoned absence of your liberty,
And patience tame to sufferance, bide each check,
Without accusing you of injury.
Be where you list, your charter is so strong
That you yourself may privilege your time
To what you will, to you it doth belong
Yourself to pardon of self-doing crime.
   I am to wait, though waiting so be hell,
   Not blame your pleasure, be it ill or well.

58

God, who first made me your slave, forbid that I should even in thought control your times of pleasure, or seek to know how you spend your hours — since I am your servant, bound to await your leisure. Being at your beck and call, let me suffer your absence, while you are free to roam, tame patience into endurance, bide every rebuke without accusing you of injury. Wherever you may be, your liberty is so entire that you may occupy your time as you will : it is your prerogative to pardon yourself of any ill you may do yourself. I am to wait, though waiting may be hell, not blame your pleasure whether good or ill.

———

The reproach is strengthened in this — and how well one recognises the situation : the older man is left to kick his heels, while the younger is off on his own. Shakespeare does not pry into what he is up to, though the impression left by the sonnet is that he is up to no good. Shakespeare recognises with his half-ironic humility, though there is reproach in the recognition — that he is Southampton's servant and has no right to expect an account of how he spends his time, though the implication of 'self-doing crime', l. 12, is that he is doing himself harm. Here again is Shakespeare's characteristic double-mindedness : there is a tutorial solicitude in the dependant's reproach.

59

If there be nothing new, but that which is
Hath been before, how are our brains beguiled,
Which, labouring for invention, bear amiss
The second burden of a former child !
O, that record could with a backward look,
Even of five hundred courses of the sun,
Show me your image in some antique book,
Since mind at first in character was done.
That I might see what the old world could say
To this composèd wonder of your frame,
Whether we are mended, or where better they,
Or whether revolution be the same.
   O, sure I am, the wits of former days
   To subjects worse have given admiring praise.

59

If there is nothing new in the world, but that which is has been before, how are our brains cheated, which — seeking to create something new — bring forth something already in existence ! O, that memory could look back five hundred years to show me your picture in some ancient book, since thought was first expressed in writing. So that I might see what an earlier world could say to this perfection of your frame : whether we have improved or they were better, or whether the cycle of years has brought us to the same point. Of one thing I am sure : the wits of former days have given praise to much worse subjects.

———

This curious and little-quoted sonnet yet tells us something about Shakespeare's attitude to his writing, and his own situation in turning out these poems. L. 3, 'labouring for invention', shows his determination to write something new. The suggestion at the back of this poem may well come from *Ecclesiastes*, i. 9 foll., 'The thing that hath been, it is that which shall be ; and that which is done is that which shall be done : and there is no new thing under the sun'.

60

Like as the waves make towards the pebbled shore
So do our minutes hasten to their end ;
Each changing place with that which goes before
In sequent toil all forwards do contend.
Nativity, once in the main of light,
Crawls to maturity, wherewith being crowned
Crooked eclipses 'gainst his glory fight,
And time that gave doth now his gift confound.
Time doth transfix the flourish set on youth
And delves the parallels in beauty's brow,
Feeds on the rarities of nature's truth,
And nothing stands but for his scythe to mow :
   And yet to times in hope my verse shall stand,
   Praising thy worth, despite his cruel hand.

60

Just as the waves make towards the pebbly shore, so our minutes
hasten onwards to their end ; each following the one before, they
move forward in sequence. Nativity, once in the centre of light,
crawls on to maturity — which, being achieved, suffers eclipse and
frustration, and time that gave now takes away. Time destroys the
bloom of youth and traces lines in the brow, feeds on nature's rarities,
and nothing stands but for his scythe to mow down. Yet my verse
in praise of you shall stand to future times, in spite of time's cruelty.

Evidently a duty-sonnet, rather conventional. The first quatrain closely
follows Golding's translation of Ovid's *Metamorphoses*, XV. 201-3 :

> As every wave drives other forth
> and that that comes behind
> Both thrusteth and is thrust itself :
> Even so the times by kind
> Do fly and follow both at once,
> and evermore renew.

Behold, however, the contrast between ordinary Elizabethan jog-trot
and Shakespeare !

61

Is it thy will thy image should keep open
My heavy eyelids to the weary night?
Dost thou desire my slumbers should be broken,
While shadows like to thee do mock my sight?
Is it thy spirit that thou send'st from thee
So far from home into my deeds to pry,
To find out shames and idle hours in me,
The scope and tenure of thy jealousy?
O no, thy love, though much, is not so great:
It is my love that keeps mine eye awake,
Mine own true love that doth my rest defeat
To play the watchman ever for thy sake.
    For thee watch I, whilst thou dost wake elsewhere,
    From me far off, with others all too near.

61

Is it your will that your image should keep me wakeful at night, that my sleep should be broken while shades of you haunt my sight? Is it your spirit that you send so far from home to pry into my deeds, to see how ill I spend my time — the aim and scope of your suspicion? No, your love is not so strong : it is my love that keeps me awake, my own true love that cheats me of my rest to play the watchman over you. I keep watch for you, while you are awake elsewhere, far off from me, with others all too near.

———

Here are the accents of sincerity, depicting a situation all too familiar : the disparity in love, as well as circumstances and fortune, between the older and the younger man. Notice in l. 7 the 'idle hours', the phrase that appears again in the dedication of *Venus and Adonis* to Southampton in 1593 : 'I vow to take advantage of all idle hours, till I have honoured you with some graver labour'.

62

Sin of self-love possesseth all mine eye,
And all my soul, and all my every part ;
And for this sin there is no remedy,
It is so grounded inward in my heart.
Methinks no face so gracious is as mine,
No shape so true, no truth of such account ;
And for myself mine own worth do define
As I all others in all worths surmount.
But when my glass shows me myself indeed,
Beated and chopped with tanned antiquity,
Mine own self-love quite contrary I read :
Self, so self-loving, were iniquity.
   'Tis thee, myself, that for myself I praise,
   Painting my age with beauty of thy days.

62

Sin of self-love possesses my eye, my mind, and every part of me ;
there is no remedy for it, it is so grounded in my heart. I think
no face more charming, no one more upright, no one so depend-
able ; in my own valuation I surpass all others. But when my
mirror shows me myself as I am, storm-beaten and chapped with
the years, I read the contradiction of any vanity : it were iniquitous
to love the self I see. It is you, my other self, that I praise in myself,
disguising my age with your youth and beauty.

———

In spite of the ingenious conceit upon which the poem is based, it is a
natural movement of the mind from the theme of disparity in love to
the disillusionment in this — all the more pathetic for being a compliment to the youthful patron in the form of undressing the older man's
vanity. However, it provides a theme for another sonnet for the patron
— and a curious one psychologically ; for Shakespeare was both modest
and had a good opinion of himself. L. 4 reflects the Prayer Book phrase,
'grafted inwardly in our hearts', which he heard in church all his days.
As for ll. 5-6, we recall Aubrey : 'He was a handsome, well-shaped man :
very good company, and of a very ready and pleasant smooth wit'.
Brief Lives, ed. A. Clark, vol. II, p. 226.

63

Against my love shall be, as I am now,
With Time's injurious hand crushed and o'er-worn ;
When hours have drained his blood and filled his brow
With lines and wrinkles ; when his youthful morn
Hath travelled on to age's steepy night,
And all those beauties whereof now he's king
Are vanishing or vanished out of sight,
Stealing away the treasure of his spring :
For such a time do I now fortify
Against confounding age's cruel knife,
That he shall never cut from memory
My sweet love's beauty, though my lover's life :
  His beauty shall in these black lines be seen,
  And they shall live, and he in them still green.

63

Against the time when my love shall be, as I am now, worn by time, when the years have drained his blood and filled his brow with lines ; when the morning of youth has moved on to the night of age, and all the charms he now commands are vanishing out of sight, the treasure of his spring consumed : for such a time do I take measures against the cruel edge of age, that it may never cut from memory my love's beauty, though it may my lover's life : his beauty shall live on in these black lines, and they will keep his memory green.

Such a relationship was bound to bring out Shakespeare's consciousness of how much older he was than the young man — practically a decade, and that meant much more then than now : the poet's life was more than half over. No doubt he had worn hard — cf. 'o'er worn', l. 2 — with his long struggle to establish himself and with his way of life. All the same, the emphasis on his age is an implied compliment to the youth of his patron. L. 5 : 'age's steepy night' refers to the course and decline of the sun in the sky.

64

When I have seen by Time's fell hand defaced
The rich, proud cost of outworn buried age ;
When sometime lofty towers I see down-razed,
And brass eternal slave to mortal rage ;
When I have seen the hungry ocean gain
Advantage on the kingdom of the shore,
And the firm soil win of the watery main,
Increasing store with loss and loss with store ;
When I have seen such interchange of state,
Or state itself confounded to decay,
Ruin hath taught me thus to ruminate,
That Time will come and take my love away.
    This thought is as a death, which cannot choose
    But weep to have that which it fears to lose.

64

When I have seen the proud monuments of the gorgeous past defaced by time, lofty towers thrown down and brasses laid for eternity ripped up by mortal fury ; when I have seen the hungry sea eating away the shore, or the land gaining upon the sea, alternating loss with gain ; when I have seen such changes of state, or states themselves brought down to decay, ruin has taught me thus to reflect, that time will take my love away also. This thought is as a death to me, since it cannot choose but lament to have that which it knows it must lose.

———

This particular group of sonnets about the ravages of time reaches its climax with this fine — and famous — one. It has historical as well as psychological interest. We can tell, from the frequent references in his works, that Shakespeare was interested by the monuments, the castles, churches, tombs, he saw as he went about the country. This, the latter half of the sixteenth century, was a sad time—like today—for a sensitive person to be travelling about England, observing the ravages wrought upon the monuments of the past. This sonnet draws our attention to the abbey-towers thrown down by the Reformation, the splendid brasses ripped out of the churches by the fury of the Reformers and the avarice of others.

The theme of land and water gaining upon each other Shakespeare derived from Golding's Ovid, which he was reading at this time for *Venus and Adonis* — it is the poem's source. Compare ll. 5-10 with Golding, *Metamorphoses*, XV. 288-90 :

> Even so have places oftentimes
> exchangèd their estate,
> For I have seen it sea which was
> substantial ground alate :
> Again where 'sea was, I have seen
> the same become dry land.

65

Since brass, nor stone, nor earth, nor boundless sea,
But sad mortality o'er-sways their power,
How with this rage shall beauty hold a plea
Whose action is no stronger than a flower?
O, how shall summer's honey breath hold out
Against the wreckful siege of battering days,
When rocks impregnable are not so stout,
Nor gates of steel so strong, but Time decays?
O fearful meditation! where, alack,
Shall Time's best jewel from Time's chest lie hid?
Or what strong hand can hold his swift foot back?
Or who his spoil of beauty can forbid?
    O, none, unless this miracle have might,
    That in black ink my love may still shine bright.

65

Since brass and stone, earth and sea, are subject to mortality, how can beauty withstand that force, when its strength is no greater than a flower's ? Or how shall the honeyed breath of summer hold out against the battering storm of time, when rocks and gates of iron are not so strong but time decays them. A fearful thought ! for where, alas, shall Time's best jewel be hid from Time's dark chest ? Or what strong hand can stay his foot ? Or who can arrest his ravages upon beauty ? None, unless there is hope in this miracle, that my love may ever shine bright out of this black ink.

An antiphon to the previous, more powerful, sonnet. It needs no comment, but we may point out how conscious Shakespeare is of the image of a jewel in a chest, cf. Sonnets 48 and 52 ; it appears in 2 *Henry VI*, III. ii. 409-10 :

> A jewel, locked into the woefull'st cask
> That ever did contain a thing of worth ;

as also in *Richard II*, and *King John*.

66

Tired with all these, for restful death I cry,
As, to behold desert a beggar born,
And needy nothing trimmed in jollity,
And purest faith unhappily forsworn,
And gilded honour shamefully misplaced,
And maiden virtue rudely strumpeted,
And right perfection wrongfully disgraced,
And strength by limping sway disabled,
And art made tongue-tied by authority,
And folly, doctor-like, controlling skill,
And simple truth miscalled simplicity,
And captive good attending captain ill :
    Tired with all these, from these would I be gone,
    Save that to die, I leave my love alone.

66

Weary with thinking of these things, I am ready to give up : to see merit born poor, for example, and the unworthy flourishing ; to see faith betrayed and bright honour put down, innocent virtue abused, perfection wrongfully demeaned ; to see strength crippled by limping power, art tongue-tied by authority, and pretentious stupidity in control of intelligence ; to see simple truth regarded as simpleness of mind, and good dancing attendance upon evil in command. Weary with all this, I would willingly be gone, except that in dying I should leave my love alone.

Here Shakespeare provides his patron with something new. This curious sonnet is most revealing : it shows the poet speaking out in his own person, Shakespeare as an Angry Man. We mark his resentment at merit being born poor, and nullity flourishing. There is a personal tone in all this, particularly the writer resenting 'art made tongue-tied by authority, and folly, doctor-like, controlling skill'. It has been thought that this was a reference to the censorship of the stage ; but it is more likely to be a generic reference to the restrictions of authority upon art and thought in all times and places, for 'art' with Shakespeare means generally the arts and sciences, letters and learning, as well as technique. At any rate, he is speaking out what he really feels in the discouraging circumstances of 1592-3, in a mood of depression and resentment. At the end, he contrives a compliment to his young patron.

Professor Richard Hosley has pointed out to me that l. 12 echoes Marlowe's

And all his captains bound in captive chains,

Tamburlaine, Part I, III. iii. 115.

67

Ah, wherefore with infection should he live
And with his presence grace impiety,
That sin by him advantage should achieve
And lace itself with his society ?
Why should false painting imitate his cheek,
And steal dead seeing of his living hue ?
Why should poor beauty indirectly seek
Roses of shadow, since his rose is true ?
Why should he live, now nature bankrupt is,
Beggared of blood to blush through lively veins ?
For she hath no exchequer now but his,
And, proud of many, lives upon his gains.
   O, him she stores, to show what wealth she had
   In days long since, before these last so bad.

67

Why should he live with these infections of the time, and grace its ills with his presence, that sin may derive advantage from him and embellish itself with his society ? Why should false painting imitate his complexion and steal a lifeless appearance from his living colour ? Why should poor beauty imitate painted roses, when his rose is natural ? Why should he live now that nature is bankrupt and beggared of blood to course through living veins ? For she has no resources now but his and, in spite of her pride, lives upon him. She stores him up, to show what wealth she once had, before these evil days.

This somewhat far-fetched sonnet continues the thought of the preceding one and develops its reflections upon the age. Shakespeare, like Spenser, disapproved of the new fashion of painting in women. It is consoling for us to find Shakespeare out of patience with his time.

68

Thus is his cheek the map of days outworn,
When beauty lived and died as flowers do now,
Before these bastard signs of fair were born,
Or durst inhabit on a living brow :
Before the golden tresses of the dead,
The right of sepulchres, were shorn away
To live a second life on second head,
Ere beauty's dead fleece made another gay :
In him those holy antique hours are seen,
Without all ornament, itself and true,
Making no summer of another's green,
Robbing no old to dress his beauty new ;
    And him as for a map doth nature store,
    To show false art what beauty was of yore.

68

And so his countenance is a pattern out of the olden time, when beauty lived and died as flowers do nowadays, before false hair was worn or dared decorate a living brow : before the tresses of the dead, the prerogative of tombs, were shorn to live again on others' heads, in days before beauty's locks made another gay. In him that ancient time is seen, without any ornament, true to itself, not decking out its summer with another's green, or robbing the old to dress up new beauty. So nature uses him as a map, to show false art what beauty was of old.

———

This subject, the shearing of locks from the dead to provide false hair for the living, gives the ingenious poet matter for another couple of sonnets for his patron. Very appropriately for Southampton, whose own golden tresses were a marked, but natural, feature. The theme is reflected not long after in *The Merchant of Venice*, III. ii. 92-6 :

> So are those crispèd, snaky, golden locks . . .
> Upon supposèd fairness, often known
> To be the dowry of a second head,
> The skull that bred them in the sepulchre.

L. 1 has a couple of reflections in *Lucrece*, l. 1712 :

> The face, that map which deep impression bears ;

and l. 1350,

> this pattern of the worn-out age.

69

Those parts of thee that the world's eye doth view
Want nothing that the thought of hearts can mend ;
All tongues, the voice of souls, give thee that due,
Uttering bare truth, even so as foes commend.
Thy outward thus with outward praise is crowned ;
But those same tongues that give thee so thine own
In other accents do this praise confound,
By seeing farther than the eye hath shown.
They look into the beauty of thy mind
And that, in guess, they measure by thy deeds ;
Then churls, their thoughts, although their eyes were kind,
To thy fair flower add the rank smell of weeds ;
   But why thy odour matcheth not thy show,
   The soil is this : that thou dost common grow.

69

Those parts of you that the world can see leave nothing that people's thought can improve on : all voices give you that due — it is but the truth that even enemies cannot deny. Thus the outer man is yielded outward praise. But those same voices mingle with it quite another accent when they look further than the eye sees. They look into your mind, measuring it in imagination by your deeds ; and so these creatures, although outwardly smiling, add the rank smell of weeds to your fair flower. But why the odour you give does not match your show, the ground is this : you make yourself common.

————

Here is a bit of straight talk of a tutorial kind from an older man to a younger, however grand. Shakespeare gives him a piece of his mind, even if wrapped up in compliments : it says much for the poet's essential independence of spirit.

70

That thou art blamed shall not be thy defect,
For slander's mark was ever yet the fair ;
The ornament of beauty is suspect,
A crow that flies in heaven's sweetest air.
So thou be good, slander doth but approve
Thy worth the greater, being wooed of time ;
For canker-vice the sweetest buds doth love,
And thou present'st a pure unstainèd prime.
Thou hast passed by the ambush of young days
Either not assailed, or victor being charged :
Yet this thy praise cannot be so thy praise,
To tie up envy evermore enlarged.
   If some suspect of ill masked not thy show,
   Then thou alone kingdoms of hearts shouldst owe.

That you are blamed is not in itself a defect, for the fair were ever the target of slander ; suspicion goes regularly along with beauty, a crow winging its way in the pure air. So long as you are good, slander only proves your worth the greater, since the time is so inviting ; for vice, like canker, likes the sweetest buds, and you offer an unstained prime. You have passed by the ambush of your earliest youth either not tempted or, if so, not having fallen : yet this just praise cannot stop envy that is always on the alert. If some blemish did not touch your appearance, then you alone would possess whole kingdoms of hearts.

———

That these sonnets are in sequence is obvious. We see again the rhythm of reproach followed by forgiveness, natural to Shakespeare : he cannot blame the young man too much. Yet we cannot but observe that reflections are beginning to be made on Southampton ; and we remember that some eighteen months later, in June 1594, that sage young lady, Lady Bridget Manners, would not consider either Southampton or the Earl of Bedford as a mate — 'they be so young, and fantastical, and would be so carried away . . . she doubteth their carriage of themselves' (*Hist. MSS. Com., Rutland*, I. 321). On Shakespeare's side we note his concern for Southampton's good. Marlowe's *Hero and Leander*, ll. 285 foll., offers a comparison with l. 2 :

> Whose name is it . . .
> So she be fair, but some vile tongues will blot ?

71

No longer mourn for me when I am dead
Than you shall hear the surly sullen bell
Give warning to the world that I am fled
From this vile world with vilest worms to dwell :
Nay, if you read this line, remember not
The hand that writ it ; for I love you so
That I in your sweet thoughts would be forgot
If thinking on me then should make you woe.
O if, I say, you look upon this verse
When I perhaps compounded am with clay,
Do not so much as my poor name rehearse,
But let your love even with my life decay :
    Lest the wise world should look into your moan,
    And mock you with me after I am gone.

When I am dead, do not mourn for me longer than you shall hear
the sullen bell give warning that I am gone from the world to dwell
with the worms.   If you read this line, do not even remember the
hand that wrote it ; for I love you so that, if thinking of me made
you grieve, I would rather be forgotten from your thoughts.   If you
should look upon these verses, when I perhaps am blended with
clay, do not even recall my name, but let your love decay with my
life ; lest the wise world should pry into your grief, and mock you
with my name after I am gone.

———

This famous poem begins a sequence in which Shakespeare turns to consider himself, the older man, in the relationship.   As always with poets, it
moves him to finer poetry.   It is perhaps natural, in the circumstances into
which the relationship has moved, that Shakespeare should write in this
mood of departure and of his own death.   This elegiac mood about themselves has always moved poets to their best efforts — Milton's 'Lycidas',
Shelley's 'Adonais', Arnold's 'Thyrsis', are even more elegies for themselves, or their lost youth, than for their dead friends.   This moving sonnet
has had its influence in subsequent literature : one hears it in the sonnets
of Christina Rossetti as in the virtual sonnet-forms of Tennyson's *In
Memoriam*.   But, with Shakespeare, there is always the actor–dramatist's
self-awareness, half playing a part, suggesting another dimension, a mirror-
world.

72

O, lest the world should task you to recite
What merit lived in me that you should love
After my death, dear love, forget me quite,
For you in me can nothing worthy prove.
Unless you would devise some virtuous lie,
To do more for me than mine own desert,
And hang more praise upon deceasèd I
Than niggard truth would willingly impart.
O, lest your true love may seem false in this,
That you for love speak well of me untrue,
My name be buried where my body is,
And live no more to shame nor me nor you.
 For I am shamed by that which I bring forth,
 And so should you, to love things nothing worth.

72

Lest the world should put you to some effort to explain what merit
there was in me that you should love on after my death, dear love,
forget me, for you can prove nothing worthy in me. Unless you
would invent some virtuous lie to do more for me than I deserve,
and devolve more praise upon me than the scant truth allows. Lest
your love seem false in speaking well of me untruly, let my name
be buried with my body and live no more to shame either me or
you. For I am ashamed of the figure I make — as you should be,
to love what is worth nothing.

This sonnet is the echo of the preceding one, and develops the theme
of what the world thinks. Where Sonnet 71 is inspired, is *donné* — in
Valéry's phrase — Sonnet 72 is made. Nevertheless, it has feeling, as
well as mastery. Notice the conciseness and the authority, in l. 1, of the
phrase, 'should task you', and in l. 13 we are given a glimpse of Shakespeare's deprecation of his own conduct, a theme which will be developed
later. Though there is something of inverted commas in Shakespeare's
self-deprecation, his writing himself down, as against his expressed confidence in his verse, there is sincerity also. It is this ambivalence, the unconscious sincerity in a completely conscious, self-aware context, that
makes the Sonnets of Shakespeare so difficult to interpret.

73

That time of year thou mayst in me behold
When yellow leaves, or none, or few, do hang
Upon those boughs which shake against the cold,
Bare, ruined choirs, where late the sweet birds sang.
In me thou see'st the twilight of such day
As after sunset fadeth in the west,
Which by and by black night doth take away,
Death's second self, that seals up all in rest.
In me thou see'st the glowing of such fire
That on the ashes of his youth doth lie
As the death-bed whereon it must expire,
Consumed with that which it was nourished by.
   This thou perceiv'st, which makes thy love more strong
   To love that well which thou must leave ere long.

73

In me you behold that time of year when a few yellow leaves or none at all hang on the branches, shaking in the cold, like bare, ruined choirs, where lately birds were singing. In me you see such twilight as there is after the sun has faded in the west, which by and by is extinguished by night — image of death, that seals up all. In me you see the glow of embers, the ashes of my youth, dying out as on a death-bed, consumed by that which fed it and gave it life. Seeing this increases your love and makes you value more that which you must take leave of before long.

This familiar and much admired sonnet offers no difficulties. 'Bare, ruined choirs' brings to the eye the roofless shells of monastic churches which stood out rawly to anyone travelling round England in the latter part of the sixteenth century ; and 'where late the sweet birds sang' carries a characteristic double suggestion of the vanished singing. This seems to be a winter sonnet, the winter of 1592-3.

74

But be contented : when that fell arrest
Without all bail shall carry me away,
My life hath in this line some interest,
Which for memorial still with thee shall stay.
When thou reviewest this, thou dost review
The very part was consecrate to thee :
The earth can have but earth, which is his due,
My spirit is thine, the better part of me :
So then thou hast but lost the dregs of life,
The prey of worms, my body being dead,
The coward conquest of a wretch's knife,
Too base of thee to be rememberèd.
   The worth of that is that which it contains,
   And that is this, and this with thee remains.

74

Be contented : when the fatal summons of death, without any appeal, carries me away, my life has some share in these lines which will remain with you for a memorial. When you look them over, you see the very part that was consecrated to you : the earth can have but earth, its due ; the spirit is yours, the better part of me. So then you will have lost but the dregs of life, the prey of worms, my body being dead, the poor victim of time, too base to be remembered by you. The worth is in what it contains, and that is my verse, which remains with you.

This is a kind of *envoi* to the preceding group, in which Shakespeare is reflecting on himself and death. What can have put this so much in mind at this moment ? It provided a theme, of course ; but also it is the natural outcome of a mood of depression, in the winter of 1592–3. We notice again the constant contrast between the modest view of himself as a man and the confidence in himself as a poet. How well justified when one thinks of the immense variety of the Sonnets, the number and facility of the variations on their theme ! No doubt Southampton was providing something in return for them.

75

So are you to my thoughts as food to life,
Or as sweet-seasoned showers are to the ground ;
And for the peace of you I hold such strife
As 'twixt a miser and his wealth is found :
Now proud as an enjoyer, and anon
Doubting the filching age will steal his treasure ;
Now counting best to be with you alone,
Then bettered that the world may see my pleasure ;
Sometime all full with feasting on your sight,
And by and by clean starvèd for a look :
Possessing or pursuing no delight,
Save what is had or must from you be took.
   Thus do I pine and surfeit day by day,
   Or gluttoning on all, or all away.

75

You are to my thoughts as food to life, or as summer showers to the ground ; and for your sake I experience the conflict between a miser and his wealth : now proud to possess it, and then fearing the thieving age will steal his treasure ; now counting it best to have you alone to myself, then proud that the world sees my delight ; sometimes full with feasting on your sight, and next clean starved for a look from you ; possessing no pleasure and pursuing none save what is had from you. And so alternately I starve and surfeit, having either everything, or else nothing at all.

───────

This little-quoted sonnet tells us a good deal. In the first place there is the gratitude of a writer — to whom everything is food for the imagination, even pain and grief — for inspiration and for a subject. Then there is the alternating pleasure and disquietude in the relationship, with perhaps the first hint that Southampton may be taken away from Shakespeare by the competition of others. 'The filching age' describes the situation aptly, for there was keen competition for a patron, when it was sometimes a question of survival for a poet. This sonnet inaugurates a new sequence, in which the literary situation becomes the dominating theme : the appearance of a rival poet on the scene, who threatens to take Shakespeare's place in his patron's favour.

76

Why is my verse so barren of new pride,
So far from variation or quick change ?
Why with the time do I not glance aside
To new-found methods and to compounds strange ?
Why write I still all one, ever the same,
And keep invention in a noted weed,
That every word doth almost tell my name,
Showing their birth and where they did proceed ?
O, know, sweet love, I always write of you,
And you and love are still my argument :
So all my best is dressing old words new,
Spending again what is already spent :
  For as the sun is daily new and old,
  So is my love still telling what is told.

76

Why is my verse devoid of new invention, without variation or change ? Why do I not follow the fashion and try new techniques and far-fetched words ? Why do I always write in the same manner, and keep to an easily recognisable style, so that every word almost tells my name and where it came from ? The reason is that I always write of you, and you and love are ever my theme : so that my best endeavour is but dressing up old words anew, spending again what has already been spent. For as the sun is both new and old every day, so my love tells over what is already told.

———

Still more informative. We see that Shakespeare held to a more tradi-tional course in the 'quick change' of verse-techniques developing in the 1590s, and thought of himself as a conservative, not one of the innovators, in the poetry of the period. We also see that by this time his own style was easily recognisable as his and 'doth almost tell my name'. His name by now was well known for his plays — witness Robert Greene's attack on him ; he had already written the three parts of *Henry VI, The Comedy of Errors, The Two Gentlemen of Verona, Titus Andronicus,* and *The Taming of the Shrew.* But, from Southampton's point of view, he might be want-ing a change by now — and in this lay some uncertainty for his poet.

77

Thy glass will show thee how thy beauties wear,
Thy dial how thy precious minutes waste ;
The vacant leaves thy mind's imprint will bear,
And of this book this learning mayst thou taste :
The wrinkles which thy glass will truly show
Of mouthèd graves will give thee memory ;
Thou by thy dial's shady stealth mayst know
Time's thievish progress to eternity.
Look, what thy memory cannot contain
Commit to these waste blanks, and thou shalt find
Those children nursed, delivered from thy brain,
To take a new acquaintance of thy mind.
   These offices, so oft as thou wilt look,
   Shall profit thee and much enrich thy book.

77

Your glass will show you how your looks wear, your pocket dial
how your time goes by ; the vacant leaves of this book you may
fill up, while from it you may learn this : the wrinkles shown in
your glass will bring to mind open graves ; by the shadow of your
dial stealing onward you may know time's thievish progress to
eternity. Commit what your memory cannot contain to these
blank pages, and you will find your thoughts — those children of
your brain — making a new impression on your mind. To consult
glass and dial will profit you : the thoughts that arise will much
enrich your book.

What an interesting sonnet, for all the conventionality of the thought.
For it shows us Shakespeare presenting Southampton with a blank book
in which to note down his thoughts, encouraging him to write — a very
tutorial frame of mind, and perhaps more characteristic of the relationship
than has been realised. It inaugurates a new sequence dominated by the
competition of other poets, one in particular, for Southampton's favour.

78

So oft have I invoked thee for my muse,
And found such fair assistance in my verse,
As every alien pen hath got my use
And under thee their poesy disperse.
Thine eyes, that taught the dumb on high to sing
And heavy ignorance aloft to fly,
Have added feathers to the learned's wing
And given grace a double majesty.
Yet be most proud of that which I compile,
Whose influence is thine and born of thee :
In other works thou dost but mend the style,
And arts with thy sweet graces gracèd be.
    But thou art all my art, and dost advance
    As high as learning my rude ignorance.

78

I have invoked you so often as my theme and found such inspiration for my verse that other pens have taken up my habit and broadcast their poetry under your protection. Your eyes, that taught dumb and ignorant me to sing, have inspired the learned and given double power to their grace. Yet be proudest of what I compose, for it is wholly born of you : in other works you serve but to improve the style, their art is graced with the graces you lend them. But you are all my art, and make my ignorance equal to learning.

This again takes us into Shakespeare's inner feeling about himself and his work. Ll. 3-4 corroborate Francis Meres' well-known reference some years later, in 1598, to the circulation of Shakespeare's 'sugared sonnets among his private friends'. He himself implies that it was this that encouraged other poets too to hope for Southampton's patronage. But the sonnet is most interesting for its confirmation of Shakespeare's consistent attitude of resentment at his own retarded beginnings, the circumstances that had made him no university wit — unlike Marlowe, Greene, Nashe, Peele, Lyly, Lodge, and so many others. He had had to make his way himself, without a university education — the significance of the reference to 'the learned'. It was literally true, ll. 13-14, that it was Southampton's friendship and the entrée to Southampton House that made all the difference. But now Shakespeare's position as Southampton's acknowledged poet is under challenge, and for him a new situation develops.

79

Whilst I alone did call upon thy aid
My verse alone had all thy gentle grace ;
But now my gracious numbers are decayed
And my sick muse doth give another place.
I grant, sweet love, thy lovely argument
Deserves the travail of a worthier pen ;
Yet what of thee thy poet doth invent
He robs thee of, and pays it thee again.
He lends thee virtue, and he stole that word
From thy behaviour ; beauty doth he give,
And found it in thy cheek ; he can afford
No praise to thee but what in thee doth live.
   Then thank him not for that which he doth say,
   Since what he owes thee thou thyself dost pay.

79

While I alone called upon your aid, my verse was alone in possessing all your grace ; but now it is losing that quality, and my muse is giving place to another. I grant, my dearest, that the theme of you is worthy of a better pen ; yet what your poet invents he takes from you : he is but paying it back. He lends you virtue — a word he stole from your behaviour ; he gives you beauty — and found it in your countenance ; he can give you no praise but what lives in you. Then you need not thank him for what he says, for what he owes you you yourself pay.

Here is the rival poet, anxious for Southampton's favour, and in a fair way to achieve it — Shakespeare refers to him as 'thy poet'. Shakespeare is ready to suggest, generously, that this man may be 'a worthier pen'. Who can this be ? But one must never forget, with the actor-poet, the 'inverted commas', the playing a conscious part — and Shakespeare's friendly nature. The rivalry may well have been friendly.

The sonnet follows convincingly upon Sonnet 78 : no need to suggest displacement, as some have done. From the aesthetic point of view notice the inspired chime of ll. 1-2, with effective repetition and internal rhyme.

80

O, how I faint when I of you do write,
Knowing a better spirit doth use your name,
And in the praise thereof spends all his might,
To make me tongue-tied, speaking of your fame !
But since your worth, wide as the ocean is,
The humble as the proudest sail doth bear,
My saucy bark, inferior far to his,
On your broad main doth wilfully appear.
Your shallowest help will hold me up afloat,
Whilst he upon your soundless deep doth ride ;
Or, being wrecked, I am a worthless boat,
He of tall building and of goodly pride.
    Then if he thrive and I be cast away,
    The worst was this : my love was my decay.

80

How I am discouraged in writing of you, knowing that a better
spirit now uses your name, and exerts all his power in praise of you
— making me tongue-tied in doing you credit ! But your worth
is wide as the ocean, and carries the humble as well as the proudest
sail : so my small boat, much inferior to his, boldly puts out on your
broad sea. Your smallest aid will keep me afloat, while he rides
secure in the soundless depths of your favour ; though, if wrecked,
I am lost, he erect and bearing up proudly. If he thrives then and I
am cast away, the worst was just that my love was my downfall.

This takes us further into the situation now developing. The rival poet
was getting ahead in Southampton's favour, and Shakespeare becoming
discouraged. For he readily admits the superiority of the 'better spirit', the
greater genius of his rival, and the ascendancy he enjoys. Shakespeare's
position is still insecure and dependent on Southampton. We perceive
how critical such a situation was, now in 1593. But who could the rival
be whose superiority of genius Shakespeare was so ready to recognise ;
and not only of genius, but of position ? For 'tall building', l. 12, is the
regular Elizabethan term for a big fine vessel, which would ride secure in
deep water, where Shakespeare's 'saucy bark', l. 7, is a light craft, in
shallow waters, easily succoured but easily wrecked. Though there is an
element of literary exaggeration in the language, and Shakespeare was
courteous and friendly by nature, we recognise that underneath the
challenge was serious.

81

Or I shall live your epitaph to make,
Or you survive when I in earth am rotten ;
From hence your memory death cannot take,
Although in me each part will be forgotten.
Your name from hence immortal life shall have,
Though I, once gone, to all the world must die :
The earth can yield me but a common grave,
When you entombèd in men's eyes shall lie.
Your monument shall be my gentle verse,
Which eyes not yet created shall o'er-read ;
And tongues-to-be your being shall rehearse,
When all the breathers of this world are dead :
  You still shall live — such virtue hath my pen —
  Where breath most breathes, even in the mouths of
  men.

81

Either I shall live to write your epitaph, or you will survive when I am laid in earth ; death cannot take your memory away from this, although everything of me will be forgotten. From this your name shall gain immortal life, though once I am gone I shall be dead to all the world : for me there is but a common grave, while you will lie recognisable in men's eyes. My verse shall be your monument, which eyes not yet created shall read over ; and tongues-to-be shall recall your being, when all those now living are dead : my pen has such power that you shall live, where breath most breathes, even in men's mouths.

———

It is natural that such a situation should call forth Shakespeare's best, and summon up his confidence in his verse, whatever diffidence he may feel about himself. The challenge spoke to his emotions, so that an inspired poem is produced, starts easily and goes straightforward with one impulse, with no difficulty, to its end envisaged from the beginning : all with simple and entire conviction. The affinity between Samuel Daniel and Shakespeare is close, and in Daniel's *Musophilus*, ll. 956 foll., we find him developing the idea in ll. 10-11.

82

I grant thou wert not married to my muse,
And therefore mayst without attaint o'er-look
The dedicated words which writers use
Of their fair subject, blessing every book.
Thou art as fair in knowledge as in hue,
Finding thy worth a limit past my praise ;
And therefore art enforced to seek anew
Some fresher stamp of the time-bettering days.
And do so, love ; yet when they have devised
What strainèd touches rhetoric can lend,
Thou, truly fair, wert truly sympathised
In true plain words by thy true-telling friend.
 And their gross painting might be better used
 Where cheeks need blood : in thee it is abused.

I grant that you were not married to my muse and so may, without complaint, overlook the words which writers dedicate to their fair subject to bring a blessing upon their works. You are as fair in knowledge as in looks, in that achieving a value beyond my praise ; therefore are you forced to seek some newer tribute from these progressive days. You may do so, dearest ; yet, when they have thought up what exaggerated touches rhetoric can lend, you, truly fair, were truly rendered in plain words by your true-telling friend. And their gross painting might be more in place where it is needed : in you it is misused.

———

From this we learn that the writers out for Southampton's favour were intellectuals. This is the meaning of the second quatrain, which implies also that Southampton wished to move with the fashion, and was flattered by their praise of his intellectual qualities. He was himself a university man, a Cambridge man — like Spenser, Marlowe, Greene, Nashe ; in 1592 he was incorporated M.A. at Oxford — like Sidney, Lyly, Peele, Lodge. Shakespeare was an outsider. All this confirms the tradition that he was, in a sense, a 'child of nature' as against the intellectuals : which does not mean that he was uneducated, nor did it prevent him — a clever grammar-school boy, more teachable than they, and with more genius — from overtaking them. Notice, in the sestet, the emphasis he gives to his own essential truth as against the strained rhetoric of others, and that, in the last couplet he speaks out with real feeling and some indignation. 'And their gross painting might be better used' is a piece of plain speaking ; nor can one fail to sense the edge in l. 8, 'Some fresher stamp of the time-bettering days'. Shakespeare did not think of himself as an intellectual or a progressive, moving with the times. He was a backward-looking man, with a dream of an older England at heart — it is a theme that comes out again and again in his plays ; he was a countryman, with country loyalties, not an urban intellectual — much cleverer than these (though he did not set store by that) ; he was romantic about Warwickshire and the Forest of Arden. He was the only one of the theatre-people who invested the earnings he made in London in his native town, which he went back to 'once a year', according to Aubrey. In this, as in some other respects, he was very different from them ; he lives on, where most of them are but studied.

Notice the emphasis that is given, as before, to Southampton's fairness, and Shakespeare's honest truth. We may in turn emphasise again this characteristic of the Sonnets : they are more true, more real, more autobiographical, than any of the literary sonnet-sequences. The subtlety is that Shakespeare's have literary touches, of course ; but — so like him — they are life, not only literature. It is beside the mark to study them as a literary sonnet-sequence, sources and all that : properly a secondary approach.

In l. 2, 'attaint' is a reference to the contemporary process of attainder for high treason — the converse of the process of impeachment, which some commentators who are not historians, adduce. Ll. 6 and 8 are difficult : I have given the sense of them.

83

I never saw that you did painting need,
And therefore to your fair no painting set ;
I found, or thought I found, you did exceed
The barren tender of a poet's debt :
And therefore have I slept in your report,
That you yourself, being extant, well might show
How far a modern quill doth come too short,
Speaking of worth, what worth in you doth grow.
This silence for my sin you did impute,
Which shall be most my glory, being dumb ;
For I impair not beauty being mute,
When others would give life and bring a tomb.
  There lives more life in one of your fair eyes
  Than both your poets can in praise devise.

83

I never thought that you needed painting, and therefore added no painting to your beauty ; I found, or thought I found, that you went beyond any offering a pcet could make you in recompense. And therefore have I been negligent in your praise, that your existence in itself might show how far a modern pen falls short in celebrating your worth. You blamed me for this silence, which is most to my credit ; for I do not impair beauty by keeping silent, when others would give life and their praise is as a tomb. There exists more life in one of your eyes than both your poets can invent.

In these sonnets we see Shakespeare reviewing his work for Southampton in the light of the new situation, that of rivalry with another poet now also in favour : 'both your poets' clearly refers to Shakespeare and the other. In the next Shakespeare tells us that Southampton was 'fond on praise', and it seems that he meant to have both poets in train. For he has reproached Shakespeare with his silence — which the poet as usual turns into matter for a poem. Shakespeare's case for his own work is that it is natural and sincere, if plain, as against the rhetoric of his brilliant rival — and the implication is that he thought it insincere. Ll. 11-12 are quite outspoken :

> For I impair not beauty being mute,
> When others would give life and bring a tomb.

84

Who is it that says most, which can say more
Than this rich praise, that you alone are you :
In whose confine immurèd is the store
Which should example where your equal grew ?
Lean penury within that pen doth dwell
That to his subject lends not some small glory ;
But he that writes of you, if he can tell
That you are you, so dignifies his story.
Let him but copy what in you is writ,
Not making worse what nature made so clear,
And such a counterpart shall fame his wit,
Making his style admirèd everywhere.
    You to your beauteous blessings add a curse,
    Being fond on praise, which makes your praises worse.

84

Who that says most can say any more than that you are yourself :
in whom is contained a store that can produce an example of
anything your equal ? It is a poor pen that does not lend some
small glory to its subject ; but he that writes of you that you are but
yourself gives dignity to his tale. Let him but copy what is written
in you, not making worse what nature made so clear, and such a
rendering shall win him fame for his wit and make his style everywhere admired. But to your blessings you add a curse, being fond
of praise, for that detracts from its value.

This duty-sonnet carries on the theme of the preceding ones, ingeniously
complimentary in their argument that Southampton needs no other praise
than that he is himself. The last couplet, which often clinches a sonnet
with something telling, emphasises the young peer's addiction to being
praised. The first quatrain gives considerable difficulty, and its punctuation has been emended by all editors since Malone. I have merely
modernised on the basis of the original, without emendation, and given
the meaning that follows — following Shakespeare's intention.

85

My tongue-tied Muse in manners holds her still,
While comments of your praise, richly compiled,
Reserve their character with golden quill
And precious phrase by all the Muses filed.
I think good thoughts, whilst other write good words,
And like unlettered clerk still cry 'Amen'
To every hymn that able spirit affords
In polished form of well-refinèd pen.
Hearing you praised, I say ''Tis so, 'tis true',
And to the most of praise add something more ;
But that is in my thought, whose love to you,
Though words come hindmost, holds his rank before.
    Then others for the breath of words respect,
    Me for my dumb thoughts, speaking in effect.

85

My tongue-tied Muse keeps decently quiet while your praises are richly sung, upholding their quality in golden letters, in exquisite phrases polished by all the Muses. I think good thoughts, whilst another writes good words, and like an illiterate parish clerk I say 'Amen' to every poem that able spirit produces in admirable form from his accomplished pen. Hearing you praised, I say ''Tis so, 'tis true', and add something more to the height of your praise — but that is in my thoughts, where my love for you comes before words. Respect, then, others for the sound of their words, but me for my dumb thoughts speaking truthfully for me.

———

This is the last sonnet to deal with the rival poet in the present tense. We need not take with absolute literalness Shakespeare's description of himself as 'tongue-tied' before the genius of the other, for he continues to turn the situation to account in verse. Nevertheless, Shakespeare is having to take second place, echoing the praises of the other 'able spirit'. No doubt the young man, avid of praise, welcomed something new and perhaps what else the newcomer had to offer. Shakespeare recognised his rival as a superior spirit : he is consistent in every reference to him in this. His claim for himself is only that he is superior in his love, in genuine devotion to the young patron. L. 3 offers some difficulty : 'reserve their character' means preserve their characteristics ; most editors have emended 'their' to 'your', but the original needs no emendation and I have kept to it. L. 9 has a parallel with *Venus and Adonis*, l. 851 :

> She says ''tis so' ; they answer all, ''tis so'.

86

Was it the proud full sail of his great verse,
Bound for the prize of all too precious you,
That did my ripe thoughts in my brain inhearse,
Making their tomb the womb wherein they grew ?
Was it his spirit, by spirits taught to write
Above a mortal pitch, that struck me dead ?
No, neither he, nor his compeers by night
Giving him aid, my verse astonishèd.
He, nor that affable familiar ghost
Which nightly gulls him with intelligence,
As victors of my silence cannot boast :
I was not sick of any fear from thence ;
    But when your countenance filled up his line,
    Then lacked I matter : that enfeebled mine.

Was it the proud full sail of his mighty verse, bound for the precious prize of much-loved you, that shut up my thoughts in my brain, leaving them there to germinate as in a tomb ? Was it his spirit, taught by spirits to write above a mortal pitch, that struck me dead ? No : neither he nor the spirits aiding him stunned my verse into silence. Neither he nor that friendly familiar that nightly gulls him with knowledge can boast that they beat me into silence : I was not discouraged by any fear from that quarter. But when your favour filled his verse, then I lacked inspiration : his enfeebled mine.

———————

With this we reach the most important of all the Sonnets autobiographically — the most difficult and the most rewarding : it enshrines a crisis in Shakespeare's life and career. Any amount of commentary has been devoted to it, mostly beside the mark. For observe that this sonnet is written in the past tense : something has suddenly happened to the rival poet ; he is not mentioned again : he has disappeared ; the rivalry is over. We can only achieve certainty from a firm chronological foundation. We have followed the Sonnets through 1592, through their references to external events and their internal coherence with *Venus and Adonis* of 1592-3. We are now in 1593. There was only one contemporary whose superiority was recognised ; only one to whom the phrase, 'the proud full sail of his great verse', could apply, confirmed by the strange particulars of this sonnet. And, by the time of this sonnet, he is dead.

Marlowe was killed in the tavern at Deptford on 30 May, and was buried there on 1 June 1593. Shakespeare had that event in mind when he wrote in *As You Like It*, III. iii. 12-13 : 'It strikes a man more dead than a

great reckoning in a little room.' In this play Shakespeare refers specific-
ally to Marlowe and quotes his famous line — the only time he quotes a
contemporary :

> Dead shepherd, now I find thy saw of might :
> 'Who ever loved that loved not at first sight ?'

We learn from the second quatrain that the rival poet dabbled with
the spirits. No one has ever satisfactorily explained ll. 9-10,

> that affable familiar ghost
> Which nightly gulls him with intelligence :

it fairly clearly refers to Mephistophilis, with his attendance on Dr. Faustus
by night. Though Marlowe was dead, his play *Dr. Faustus* — in which
Faustus is very much a projection of Marlowe — continued to be per-
formed. Thus the present tense of 'nightly gulls him with intelligence'
is in place in this sonnet in the past tense.

And we can now explain the previous ll. 7-8, which have hitherto
resisted interpretation : 'his compeers by night giving him aid' is usually
taken to refer to the corporeal night-companions of the rival poet. We
now perceive that — so characteristic of Shakespeare — it is simply another way of expressing the idea in the previous ll. 5-6, 'by spirits taught
to write above a mortal pitch'.

What would have happened to Shakespeare in this crisis for him,
dependent as he was on Southampton, had Marlowe not been killed ?
We have seen from the Introduction that Marlowe was writing his *Hero
and Leander*, describing Southampton in the guise of Leander, in competition with Shakespeare's *Venus and Adonis*, in which Southampton is Adonis.
Shakespeare's poem came out in the month before Marlowe died, leaving
his poem uncompleted.

87

Farewell ! thou art too dear for my possessing,
And like enough thou know'st thy estimate :
The charter of thy worth gives thee releasing,
My bonds in thee are all determinate.
For how do I hold thee but by thy granting,
And for that riches where is my deserving ?
The cause of this fair gift in me is wanting,
And so my patent back again is swerving.
Thyself thou gav'st, thy own worth then not knowing,
Or me, to whom thou gav'st it, else mistaking ;
So thy great gift, upon misprision growing,
Comes home again, on better judgment making.
   Thus have I had thee, as a dream doth flatter,
   In sleep a king, but waking no such matter.

87

Farewell ! you are too dear for me to possess you, and likely enough you know your own value : your very worth releases you, my claims upon you are at an end. For how can I hold you but by your own grant, and how should I deserve that good fortune ? There is no cause in me for such a gift, and so my privilege comes back to me. You gave yourself, not knowing your own worth, or else mistaking me to whom you gave it. And so your great gift, based on a mis-understanding, comes home again, on better consideration. So I have possessed you as in a flattering dream, thinking myself a king, and waking up to find no such thing.

————

This sonnet reads like a conclusion to the previous section dominated by the rivalry with Marlowe. In it Shakespeare seems to take a contingent leave — though making a poem out of it, turning the material of the experience to use. Ingenious as ever, here he plays variations on images from the law — 'bonds ... determinate', 'charter ... releasing', 'patent', 'misprision', which means oversight or mistake, 'grant', and even 'gift'.

Observe the melancholy, farewell effect of all the feminine endings of the line in present participles, no less than ten out of fourteen lines. Psychologically, notice the double suggestion in the word 'dear' in l. 1, meaning both too much beloved and too costly, and the piece of realism without illusion of l. 2,

> And like enough thou know'st thy estimate.

Light is thrown on the origin of the relationship by ll. 9-10 :

> Thyself thou gav'st, thy own worth then not knowing,
> Or me, to whom thou gav'st it, else mistaking.

Southampton as a youth had made a friend of the poet whom he had taken on ; l. 10 has the interesting suggestion that he may have mistaken his man : there was in Shakespeare an essential independence.

88

When thou shalt be disposed to set me light
And place my merit in the eye of scorn,
Upon thy side against myself I'll fight
And prove thee virtuous, though thou art forsworn.
With mine own weakness being best acquainted,
Upon thy part I can set down a story
Of faults concealed, wherein I am attainted,
That thou in losing me shalt win much glory :
And I by this will be a gainer too :
For bending all my loving thoughts on thee,
The injuries that to myself I do,
Doing thee vantage, double-vantage me.
    Such is my love, to thee I so belong,
    That for thy right myself will bear all wrong.

88

When you shall be disposed to regard me lightly and write down my worth to little value, I will contend on your side against myself and prove you upright, although faithless. Since I am best acquainted with my own weakness, on your behalf I can set down a tale of concealed faults, of which I am guilty, so that in losing me you shall be a gainer. And so shall I be too, for, directing all my thoughts on you, the injuries I do myself, in profiting you, will be of double profit to me. Such is my love, and so much do I belong to you, that to make you right I will bear all wrong.

––––––––––

After the strain between Shakespeare and his young patron over Marlowe, there is the implied reproach against Southampton's regarding him lightly, contingently exposing his worth to others' scorn — *i.e.* by letting him down. The implication that Southampton might be 'forsworn' is not a pleasant one, a stricture in spite of the protestations of love in which it is wrapped up.

89

Say that thou didst forsake me for some fault,
And I will comment upon that offence ;
Speak of my lameness, and I straight will halt,
Against thy reasons making no defence.
Thou canst not, love, disgrace me half so ill,
To set a form upon desirèd change,
As I'll myself disgrace ; knowing thy will,
I will acquaintance strangle and look strange ;
Be absent from thy walks ; and in my tongue
Thy sweet belovèd name no more shall dwell,
Lest I, too much profane, should do it wrong,
And haply of our old acquaintance tell.
    For thee, against myself I'll vow debate,
    For I must ne'er love him whom thou dost hate.

89

Say that you forsook me for some fault — and I will confess to the offence ; say that I am lame, and immediately I will be so, putting up no defence against your attitude. Dearest, you cannot disgrace me half so much, to give a pretext for a change you wish for, as I will disgrace myself. Knowing your will, I will deny acquaintance and appear a stranger ; keep away from where you resort ; I will call no more upon your loved name, lest my common tongue should do it wrong and perhaps speak of our old acquaintance. I'll take up the debate against myself for you, since I must never love him whom you hate.

This carries forward Shakespeare's reflection upon the strain the relationship has undergone — with the references to the possibility of Southampton's parting with him, giving a pretext for a desired change.

Phrases are reflected later in the plays. L. 6, 'to set a form', reappears in *King John*, V. vii. 26 ; l. 14 is virtually repeated in *Much Ado*, V. ii. 71, 'for I will never love that which my friend hates'. We are reminded of another aspect of the Sonnets — as a workshop for the plays, where complex personal relations and their expression were first worked out.

90

Then hate me when thou wilt ; if ever, now :
Now while the world is bent my deeds to cross,
Join with the spite of fortune, make me bow,
And do not drop in for an after-loss.
Ah, do not, when my heart hath 'scaped this sorrow,
Come in the rearward of a conquered woe ;
Give not a windy night a rainy morrow,
To linger out a purposed overthrow.
If thou wilt leave me, do not leave me last,
When other petty griefs have done their spite,
But in the onset come : so shall I taste
At first the very worst of fortune's might.
   And other strains of woe, which now seem woe,
   Compared with loss of thee will not seem so.

90

Then hate me when you will : if ever, now. Now, while the world is bent on crossing me, join in with the spite of fortune, and beat me down : do not come in with an after-blow. When my heart has recovered from one grief, do not come afterward with another, like a rainy day after a night of storm, to let me linger in disgrace already decided on. If you will leave me, do not leave me at the end, when other griefs have already worn me down ; but come at the outset — so that I shall feel the worst of my fate at the beginning. Then other causes for grief which now seem bad enough, compared with losing you, will not seem so.

The relationship has become uneasy, never the same after the breach of trust over the mistress, still more over the rival poet. What is in question is whether Southampton will continue his favour and go on supporting his poet at this critical juncture, with the theatres continuing to be closed to the end of this year, 1593. This is the meaning of the reiterated emphasis on the 'spite of fortune', 'a purposed overthrow'. We have noted how much Shakespeare resented the ill-fortune of his beginnings ; now, when by 1592 he had achieved recognition and his plays were successful, the theatres were closed for most of these two plague years, 1592 and 1593, badly hitting him as both actor and dramatist dependent on them. How was he to live ? How was he living ? We have reason to suppose — to some extent on his patron's bounty. There can be no doubt about the seriousness of the matter — one hears its accents, anxiety, resentment, grief, in these Sonnets. In the midst of it all, one cannot but point out the naturalness of expression, the countryman's image, l. 7,

Give not a windy night a rainy morrow —

so unlike Marlowe.

91

Some glory in their birth, some in their skill,
Some in their wealth, some in their bodies' force ;
Some in their garments, though new-fangled ill,
Some in their hawks and hounds, some in their horse.
And every humour hath his adjunct pleasure,
Wherein it finds a joy above the rest ;
But these particulars are not my measure :
All these I better in one general best.
Thy love is better than high birth to me,
Richer than wealth, prouder than garments' cost,
Of more delight than hawks or horses be ;
And, having thee, of all men's pride I boast :
   Wretched in this alone, that thou mayst take
   All this away and me most wretched make.

91

Some people take pride in their birth, some in their skill, some in wealth, some in strength of body ; some take pride in their clothes, fashionable though ill-becoming, some people in their hawks and hounds, others in their horses. Each temperament has its particular pleasure, which it enjoys above any other. But these individual tastes are not my line : I better them all in one best of all. To me your love is better than high birth, richer than wealth, prouder than the costliest clothes, of more delight than horses, hawks or hounds ; and having you, I boast of having more than all of them. I am wretched only in this, that you may take all this away and make me miserable.

————

This more relaxed little poem follows naturally enough on the heels of the previous, more urgent, one. Nevertheless, the apprehension remains and is given full expression in the concluding couplet, which is indeed the *clou* of the poem. It offers no difficulty, except in l. 3, 'new-fangled ill' : the Elizabethan phrase, new-fangled, which means new-fashioned, is still sometimes heard in country places. 'New-fangled ill' means fashionably unattractive. The phrase is consistent with Shakespeare's old-fashioned country tastes : we have already seen that he did not much care for new fashions, the taste for cosmetics, etc.

92

But do thy worst to steal thyself away,
For term of life thou art assurèd mine ;
And life no longer than thy love will stay,
For it depends upon that love of thine.
Then need I not to fear the worst of wrongs,
When in the least of them my life hath end ;
I see a better state to me belongs
Than that which on thy humour doth depend.
Thou canst not vex me with inconstant mind,
Since that my life on thy revolt doth lie :
O, what a happy title do I find,
Happy to have thy love, happy to die !
    But what's so blessèd-fair that fears no blot ?
    Thou mayst be false, and yet I know it not.

92

Do your worst to steal yourself away from me, yet you are mine for the term of my life ; my life will last no longer than your love, for it depends wholly upon it. So then I need not fear the worst of wrongs, when in the least of them I can make an end : a better state exists for me than that which depends on your humour. You cannot torment me with your inconstancy, since my life depends on your friendship. O, what a right to be happy I have — happy to have your love, or else happy to die ! But what is so fortunate that fears no mishap ? You may be false, and I not know it.

———

What a revealing sonnet this is ! I do not think that its gravity, in the circumstances, has ever been grasped. It tells us quite clearly that Shakespeare's life will last no longer than Southampton's love, that it will come to an end with it. Things were as serious as that with Shakespeare in 1592-3. There was nothing remote in the idea of the death of a poet in those cruel years : indeed there was a high mortality among poets. In 1592 Thomas Watson and Robert Greene died ; in 1593 Marlowe, in the winter of 1593-4 Kyd, then Peele. What matter if one more were added to them ? There is the implication of the resigned tone of this sonnet, with Shakespeare accepting his fate either way. But what a shock it gives one to realise that he might have died in 1593, as well as Marlowe — and with all the work by which he lives unaccomplished ! There is reproach in ll. 8-9 — Shakespeare's understandable resentment at depending on a young man's humour, who had given evidence of his inconstancy in turning to Marlowe. In l. 10 the idea is carried on in the word 'revolt', which is cognate with revolution : the line means, literally 'since my life lies on your revolving round'.

93

So shall I live, supposing thou art true,
Like a deceivèd husband ; so love's face
May still seem love to me, though altered new :
Thy looks with me, thy heart in other place.
For there can live no hatred in thine eye,
Therefore in that I cannot know thy change :
In many's looks the false heart's history
Is writ in moods and frowns and wrinkles strange.
But heaven in thy creation did decree
That in thy face sweet love should ever dwell ;
Whate'er thy thoughts, or thy heart's workings be,
Thy looks should nothing thence but sweetness tell.
   How like Eve's apple doth thy beauty grow,
   If thy sweet virtue answer not thy show !

93

So shall I continue like a deceived husband, supposing you to be true ; so love's face may still seem love to me, though really altered : your looks with me, your heart elsewhere. For no hatred can exist in your eye, so that I cannot know your change by that : with most people the false heart betrays itself in their looks, in moods and frowns and unfriendly countenance. But heaven in creating you decreed that your face should express love ; whatever your thoughts or your heart's workings might be, your looks speak nothing but sweetness. Your beauty would be a perfect Eve's apple if your goodness did not answer your appearance.

———

After an extremely serious sonnet, a lighter one : such is the rhythm. But the apprehension continues, and after the doubt, the fear of Southampton's turning away, things could hardly be the same. Still, what a tribute is paid to the young man's essential sweetness of nature in this sonnet : in the end his well-known generosity and loyalty came through and was fully borne out.

94

They that have power to hurt and will do none,
That do not do the thing they most do show,
Who, moving others, are themselves as stone,
Unmovèd, cold, and to temptation slow :
They rightly do inherit heaven's graces
And husband nature's riches from expense ;
They are the lords and owners of their faces,
Others but stewards of their excellence.
The summer's flower is to the summer sweet,
Though to itself it only live and die,
But if that flower with base infection meet,
The basest weed outbraves his dignity :
    For sweetest things turn sourest by their deeds,
    Lilies that fester smell far worse than weeds.

94

They that have power to hurt yet do not do it, that do not do what they give the appearance of doing, who attract others though they themselves are cold and unmoved, slow to temptation.: they rightly inherit heaven's graces, preserving nature's riches from waste ; they are the owners of themselves, where others are but caretakers of their endowments. The summer's flower is sweet, though it lives and dies only for itself ; but if it becomes cankered the coarsest weed surpasses it. For sweetest things turn sourest by what they do ; lilies that rot smell far worse than weeds.

––––––––––

This curious and powerful sonnet has a cutting edge to it. There is no reason to suppose that it is out of place, as has often been suggested : it continues the theme announced at the end of the previous sonnet — the doubt whether Southampton's virtue matched his outward appearance, and it links up with the next sonnet in which the doubt is confirmed, the reason made explicit. Is Shakespeare implying that Southampton is one of those

> Who, moving others, are themselves as stone ?

Likely enough : he would not give himself to marriage ; his flirtation with Shakespeare's mistress was a much more superficial affair than the poet's passionate involvement ; later we know that he wished to get out of marrying Elizabeth Vernon. It is apparent that there was a good deal of narcissism in his make-up ; this is reflected in the theme and images of *Venus and Adonis* as throughout the Sonnets. Indeed it is the subject of the first section, 1-26.

L. 14 appears also in Peele's *Edward III*, II. i. 452 : an Elizabethan commonplace.

95

How sweet and lovely dost thou make the shame
Which, like a canker in the fragrant rose,
Doth spot the beauty of thy budding name !
O, in what sweets dost thou thy sins enclose !
That tongue that tells the story of thy days,
Making lascivious comments on thy sport,
Cannot dispraise but in a kind of praise :
Naming thy name blesses an ill report.
O, what a mansion have those vices got,
Which for their habitation chose out thee,
Where beauty's veil doth cover every blot
And all things turn to fair that eyes can see !
    Take heed, dear heart, of this large privilege :
    The hardest knife ill-used doth lose his edge.

95

How beguiling you make the shame, which, like blight in a rose, spots the perfection of your budding name. O, in what an envelope you enclose your sins ! The very tongue that reports how you spend your days, with malicious comments on your sport, cannot dispraise you but in a kind of praise : naming your name makes an ill report good. What a mansion those blemishes have which chose you for their habitation, where your looks cover every blot and give everything a fair appearance ! Take heed, dear heart, of this large liberty you have : the hardest knife loses it edge with ill use.

Here is the tutorial attitude towards the young man with a vengeance, nor need we have much doubt about the activities — the 'sins', l. 4, the 'vices', l. 9 — that disinclined him from marriage. L. 8 recalls the phrasing of Nashe's tribute to Spenser, in his *Strange News* of 1592 : 'his very name (as that of Ned Allen on the common stage) was able to make an ill matter good'. Shakespeare knew and read Nashe. Observe the internal rhymes in ll. 9-10, 'those' and 'chose', and the simple image of the last line, true to a man of the people.

96

Some say thy fault is youth, some wantonness,
Some say thy grace is youth and gentle sport ;
Both grace and faults are loved of more and less :
Thou mak'st faults graces that to thee resort.
As on the finger of a thronèd queen
The basest jewel will be well esteemed :
So are those errors that in thee are seen
To truths translated and for true things deemed.
How many lambs might the stern wolf betray,
If like a lamb he could his looks translate !
How many gazers mightst thou lead away,
If thou wouldst use the strength of all thy state !
   But do not so : I love thee in such sort
   As, thou being mine, mine is thy good report.

96

Some say that your fault is youth and some frivolousness, others that youth and sport are graces in you ; both grace and faults are loved alike by great and small : you make faults that capture you into graces. As the poorest jewel on the finger of a queen will be well thought of, so your errors are turned into qualities and taken as such. How many lambs might the wolf deceive if he could turn himself into the likeness of a lamb ! How many admirers might you lead astray, if you were to use all the power of your rank and state ! But do not do this : I love you so much that, as you are mine, mine is your good repute.

The tutorial note continues, and how closely this is borne out by Lady Bridget Manners's objection to Southampton for a husband as 'so young and fantastical and would be so carried away' (cf. my *Shakespeare's Southampton*, 98.)

In ll. 5-6 Shakespeare had Queen Elizabeth in mind : one sees a flicker of the actor-dramatist performing before her, catching sight of a jewel. The concluding couplet is repeated from Sonnet 36 : evidently the lines had so impressed themselves in his mind — an indication of how significant this way of thinking was to him in the relationship. Such a repetition, along with the misprints, indicates that Shakespeare was not responsible for the eventual publication of the Sonnets.

97

How like a winter hath my absence been
From thee, the pleasure of the fleeting year !
What freezings have I felt, what dark days seen !
What old December's bareness everywhere !
And yet this time removed was summer's time,
The teeming autumn, big with rich increase,
Bearing the wanton burden of the prime,
Like widowed wombs after their lords' decease :
Yet this abundant issue seemed to me
But hope of orphans and unfathered fruit ;
For summer and his pleasures wait on thee
And, thou away, the very birds are mute ;
   Or, if they sing, 'tis with so dull a cheer
   That leaves look pale, dreading the winter's near.

How like winter has my absence from you been, the delight of the year now fleeting away ! How frozen I have felt, what dark days been through, the bareness of December around one everywhere ! And yet the previous time of absence was in summer and teeming autumn, heavy with fruitfulness, bearing the burden of the spring, like widows left with child by their lords. Yet all this fruitfulness seemed to me as if orphaned and unfathered : for summer and its pleasures wait on you and, with you away, the very birds are silent. Or, if they sing, it is with so little spirit that the leaves look pale, dreading the approach of winter.

———

This sonnet begins a new group, written in absence and, as it would appear, with the winter of 1593 ahead. In l. 5, 'this time removed' has an active sense, and would mean the previous time when Shakespeare was removed from being with or near Southampton : it seems then to refer to an absence during the summer and early autumn of 1592. Commentators have found difficulty with both the argument and the imagery. The argument is simple : absence from Southampton, whether in the approach of winter as now, or in summer and early autumn as before, makes Shakespeare sad. The different seasons have somewhat confused the imagery. L. 7 : 'the wanton burden of the prime' I have taken to refer to spring, when the fruits were wantonly, i.e. playfully, conceived ; but it might refer to harvest.

98

From you have I been absent in the spring,
When proud-pied April, dressed in all his trim,
Hath put a spirit of youth in every thing,
That heavy Saturn laughed and leaped with him.
Yet nor the lays of birds, nor the sweet smell
Of different flowers in odour and in hue,
Could make me any summer's story tell,
Or from their proud lap pluck them where they grew :
Nor did I wonder at the lily's white,
Nor praise the deep vermilion in the rose ;
They were but sweet, but figures of delight
Drawn after you, you pattern of all those.
   Yet seemed it winter still, and you away,
   As with your shadow I with these did play.

98

I have been absent from you in spring, when April, in all its coloured bravery, has put such a youthful spirit in everything that even heavy Saturn laughed and leaped. Yet neither the song of birds, nor the fragrance of flowers in their many colours, could make me tell a summer's tale, or pick the flowers from where they grew on the proud earth. Nor did I wonder at the white of the lily, nor praise the redness of the rose : they were but images of delight drawn after you, pattern of all of them. For it seemed winter still, with you away, as I played with these shadows of you.

It is not necessary to suppose, as some have done, that because this refers to a different absence in spring, the sonnet is misplaced. The point is that it continues the theme of absence, and though referring back to another separation in spring, is likely to have been written along with this group in the early winter of 1593. We have observed before how much and how often Shakespeare is away from Southampton : they would not have seen so much of each other as people suppose who do not know the circumstances of the age.

L. 7 refers to the intention of telling a summer's story, and thus to the germination of *A Midsummer Night's Dream*, which was produced for the marriage of the Countess of Southampton, 2 May 1594. L. 4 : the influence of Saturn was supposed to be gloomy and heavy — hence saturnine.

99

The forward violet thus did I chide :
Sweet thief, whence didst thou steal thy sweet that smells
If not from my love's breath ? The purple pride
Which on thy soft cheek for complexion dwells
In my love's veins thou hast too grossly dyed.
The lily I condemnèd for thy hand,
And buds of marjoram had stol'n thy hair ;
The roses fearfully on thorns did stand,
One blushing shame, another white despair ;
A third, nor red nor white, had stol'n of both,
And to his robbery had annexed thy breath ;
But, for his theft, in pride of all his growth
A vengeful canker ate him up to death.
   More flowers I noted, yet I none could see
   But sweet or colour it had stol'n from thee.

99

Thus did I chide the too early violet : Sweet thief, whence did you steal your fragrance, if not from my love's breath ? The purple of your complexion you have too grossly drawn from my love's veins. The lily I condemned compared with the whiteness of your hand, and buds of marjoram had stolen their colour from your hair ; the roses stood uneasily on thorns, one blushing shame, another white with despair ; a third, neither red nor white, had filched colour of both and added the fragrance of your breath ; but for his theft, in the pride of life a canker-worm ate him up in revenge. I noted still more flowers, but I could see none that had not stolen fragrance or colour from you.

This piece has a charming artificiality : it is an ingenious exercise in compliment, like the poems the poets of the early 1590s wrote to their ladies. But its literary interest is greater, for it is irregular — it has fifteen lines. It has been suggested that it is an unfinished draft, not properly reduced to shape. I do not think so ; for, notice, the first line is a prelude, an announcement ; then follows the sonnet. Ll. 5-6 are not easy, for they are elliptical and open to alternative interpretations. L. 7 would seem to indicate that Southampton's hair, a golden auburn in his portraits, curled naturally. There are parallels to l. 13 in both *Venus and Adonis*, 656, and *Romeo and Juliet*, II. iii. 30.

100

Where art thou, Muse, that thou forget'st so long
To speak of that which gives thee all thy might ?
Spend'st thou thy fury on some worthless song,
Dark'ning thy power to lend base subjects light ?
Return, forgetful Muse, and straight redeem
In gentle numbers time so idly spent ;
Sing to the ear that doth thy lays esteem
And gives thy pen both skill and argument.
Rise, resty Muse, my love's sweet face survey,
If Time have any wrinkle graven there ;
If any, be a satire to decay,
And make Time's spoils despisèd everywhere.
   Give my love fame faster than Time wastes life,
   So thou prevent'st his scythe, and crooked knife.

Some time has elapsed since Shakespeare wrote last. Fairly certainly
written — like all this group — in absence, the sonnet's theme is the effect
of time, during this interval, upon the young patron. Looking for the
truth of fact under the proper form for complimentary verse in those
days, we are struck by the truth of l. 2. Many have noticed the marked
contrast between Shakespeare's first, artificial comedies, *The Comedy of
Errors* and *The Two Gentlemen of Verona*, and the work that is connected
with the Sonnets, *A Midsummer Night's Dream, Love's Labour's Lost, Romeo
and Juliet* : a difference has been made by the intervening experience
of life, the inspiration of love, with its accompanying exaltation and
anguish, a dimension added to life. We must also attend to the literal
truth of ll. 7-8 ; we learn that Southampton appreciated Shakespeare's
poetry. And now there is no rival for favour ; there is a relaxed tone
in these sonnets : Shakespeare, like his Muse, is taking things more easily.
Moreover, in 1593, there was the marked success as a poet that he achieved

Where are you, my Muse, that you forget so long to speak of that which gives you all your power ? Do you waste your energy on some worthless theme, lowering your powers to light up some base subject ? Forgetful Muse, return and redeem in verse the time you have spent so idly ; sing to him who esteems your poetry, and gives your pen both skill and theme. Rise, slothful Muse, look into my love's countenance to see if Time has graven any furrow there ; if so, turn your satire against decay and make Time's ravages every-where despised. Give my love fame faster than Time wastes away life, so that you get in before his scythe mows down.

───────

with *Venus and Adonis*. Ll. 3-4 give us Shakespeare's comment on what has been occupying him — writing plays, instead of poetry on a noble theme, *i.e.* to Southampton.

The easy, relaxed tone of these sonnets brings to mind the early tradition, coming through Davenant, that Southampton gave Shakespeare a handsome present 'to enable him to go through with a purchase which . . . he had a mind to' (cf. E. K. Chambers, vol. II. pp. 266-7). It is thought that it was this that enabled him to acquire a share in the Lord Chamberlain's company when it was formed in 1594, and this gave him financial security at last.

It would be appropriate, indeed expected, for an Elizabethan patron to mark the dedications of *Venus and Adonis* and *Lucrece* with a gift ; and that gives us, for our dating, precisely 1593 and 1594.

101

O truant Muse, what shall be thy amends
For thy neglect of truth in beauty dyed ?
Both truth and beauty on my love depends ;
So dost thou too, and therein dignified.
Make answer, Muse : wilt thou not haply say,
'Truth needs no colour, with his colour fixed ;
Beauty no pencil, beauty's truth to lay ;
But best is best, if never intermixed' ?
Because he needs no praise, wilt thou be dumb ?
Excuse not silence so, for't lies in thee
To make him much outlive a gilded tomb
And to be praised of ages yet to be.
   Then do thy office, Muse : I teach thee how
   To make him seem long hence as he shows now.

O truant Muse, what amends will you make for your neglect of truth-in-beauty ? Both truth and beauty depend on my love ; so do you too, and are the nobler for it. Make answer, Muse : will you not perhaps say, 'Truth needs no colouring, set down as it is with his colour ; beauty needs no pencil, to lay on truth ; each is best alone, without any mixture'? Because he needs no praise, will you be silent ? Excuse it not thus, for it lies in you to make him out-live a gilded tomb and be praised by ages yet to come. Then do your duty, Muse : I teach you how to make him appear long hence as he appears now.

This continues the new turn Shakespeare gives to the theme, turning his silence, at any rate his writing less frequently, to account poetically. Naturally, after so many offerings, there is some repetition : ll. 10-12 repeat the argument of the famous Sonnet 55 and others. In ll. 1-2, notice the echo of 'truant' and 'truth'. So ingenious a master can permit himself the monosyllabic simplicity, the casual colloquialism, of the last line ; a less naturally gifted writer, of course, not.

102

My love is strengthened though more weak in seeming,
I love not less, though less the show appear ;
That love is merchandized whose rich esteeming
The owner's tongue doth publish everywhere.
Our love was new, and then but in the spring,
When I was wont to greet it with my lays ;
As Philomel in summer's front doth sing,
And stops her pipe in growth of riper days :
Not that the summer is less pleasant now
Than when her mournful hymns did hush the night,
But that wild music burdens every bough,
And sweets grown common lose their dear delight.
    Therefore, like her, I sometimes hold my tongue,
    Because I would not dull you with my song.

102

My love is confirmed, though it appears less so ; in spite of appearances I do not love less : that love is cheapened whose value is everywhere extolled by the owner. Our love was new and but at the beginning when I used to greet it with my poems : as the nightingale sings in early summer, and ceases as the summer wears on. Not that the season is less pleasant now than when her mournful melody hushed the night, but that birdsong now burdens every bough, and delights grown common lose their appeal. Therefore, like her, I am sometimes silent, because I would not bore you with my verse.

This turn of the theme is continued, in a relaxed, appeased mood. We learn something valuable : that the Sonnets began, it would seem from the imagery, in the spring, of 1592. We learn further, from l. 11, of the increase of this kind of poetry, of the sonnet vogue, in these years. The tone is retrospective, beginning to look back over the course of the friendship.

Ll. 3-4 have a parallel in *Love's Labour's Lost*, II. i. 15-16 :

> Beauty is bought by judgment of the eye,
> Not uttered by base sale of chapmen's tongues.

103

Alack, what poverty my Muse brings forth,
That having such a scope to show her pride
The argument, all bare, is of more worth
Than when it hath my added praise beside.
O, blame me not, if I no more can write !
Look in your glass and there appears a face
That over-goes my blunt invention quite,
Dulling my lines and doing me disgrace.
Were it not sinful then, striving to mend,
To mar the subject that before was well ?
For to no other pass my verses tend
Than of your graces and your gifts to tell.
    And more, much more, than in my verse can sit,
    Your own glass shows you when you look in it.

103

Alas, what a poor show my Muse puts up, that having such scope to prove her mettle, the subject in itself is worth more than when my praise is added to it. Do not blame me if I can write no more ! Look in your glass and you will see a face that goes quite beyond my blunt invention, making my lines dull and doing me discredit. Isn't it a mistake then, in striving to improve, to mar the subject that was very well before ? For my verses tend to no other end than to celebrate your gifts and graces. And when you look in your own glass it shows much more than there can be in my verse.

———

This shows Shakespeare conscious of coming to the end of his inspiration. After all, of this kind of verse there must some time come an end, and here he is repeating himself : we have had all that about the glass before, cf. Sonnet 77, for example. Even so, he turns his apology to account : matter for yet another offering, if not a very good one, to an expectant patron.

104

To me, fair friend, you never can be old,
For as you were when first your eye I eyed,
Such seems your beauty still : three winters cold
Have from the forests shook three summers' pride,
Three beauteous springs to yellow autumn turned
In process of the seasons have I seen,
Three April perfumes in three hot Junes burned,
Since first I saw you fresh, which yet are green.
Ah, yet doth beauty like a dial-hand
Steal from his figure, and no pace perceived ;
So your sweet hue, which methinks still doth stand,
Hath motion, and mine eye may be deceived :
    For fear of which, hear this, thou age unbred :
    Ere you were born was beauty's summer dead.

104

To me, my friend, you never can be old, for as you were when I first beheld you, such is your beauty still : three winters have shaken three summers' foliage from the forests, three springs have I seen turn to autumn in the procession of the seasons, three April perfumes burned up in three hot Junes, since first I saw you — and you are yet young. Still beauty moves on, like a dial-hand stealing forward and no movement seen ; so your looks, which seem to me unchanged, have motion, and my eye may be deceived. For fear of which, hear this, you age unborn : before ever you came into being beauty's summer was dead.

———

It is almost impossible to render this wonderful sonnet in any terms other than its own. Continuing this theme, the passage of time, Shakespeare has at length found inspiration in looking back nostalgically over the three years of the friendship to its beginning. So that gives us a date : we are now in the summer of 1594. The three winters of the friendship are those of 1591-2, 1592-3, 1593-4 ; the Aprils and Junes are those of 1592, 1593, 1594. Southampton was now twenty — he would be twenty-one and reach his majority in October 1594 — and was as beautiful as he had been at eighteen. But the dial-hand was moving on, as in Sonnet 77, and Shakespeare, now thirty, was repeating himself.

L. 4 is reflected in *Romeo and Juliet*, I. ii. 10 ;

> Let two more summers wither in their pride.

The image in l. 7, derived from burning perfumes in a house, reflects Shakespeare's increased sophistication with his acquaintance with high society and great houses.

105

Let not my love be called idolatry,
Nor my belovèd as an idol show,
Since all alike my songs and praises be
To one, of one, still such, and ever so.
Kind is my love today, tomorrow kind,
Still constant in a wondrous excellence ;
Therefore my verse to constancy confined,
One thing expressing, leaves out difference.
'Fair, kind, and true', is all my argument,
'Fair, kind, and true', varying to other words ;
And in this change is my invention spent,
Three themes in one, which wondrous scope affords.
  'Fair, kind, and true', have often lived alone,
  Which three till now never kept seat in one.

105

Let not my love be called idolatry, nor my beloved appear as an idol, because all my poems are written to one, of one, are still so and always will be. My love is kind today, as he will be tomorrow, ever constant in excellence ; therefore my verse is confined to constancy, expressing only one thing, leaving out all variation. 'Fair, kind, and true', is my whole theme, 'fair, kind, and true', sometimes in other words : my invention is spent in ringing these changes, three themes in one, affording infinite scope. 'Fair, kind, and true', have often existed separately, but never till now were all found in one.

———

This conventional enough sonnet still tells us something very important to know — that all Shakespeare's poems were written to and for Southampton, were about him and would continue to be so. This is, of course, a poet's exaggeration ; but it serves to bring home to us that Shakespeare, unlike Jonson and others, had only one patron, acknowledged in the dedications of his two poems, and no other.

106

When in the chronicle of wasted time
I see descriptions of the fairest wights,
And beauty making beautiful old rhyme
In praise of ladies dead and lovely knights,
Then in the blazon of sweet beauty's best,
Of hand, of foot, of lip, of eye, of brow,
I see their antique pen would have expressed
Even such a beauty as you master now.
So all their praises are but prophecies
Of this our time, all you prefiguring ;
And, for they looked but with divining eyes,
They had not still enough your worth to sing :
   For we, which now behold these present days,
   Have eyes to wonder, but lack tongues to praise.

106

When in chronicles of past time I see descriptions of the fairest persons, and old rhyme made beautiful by praise of dead ladies and handsome knights — then in beauty's best scutcheon, of hand and foot, of lip and eye and brow, I see their pens of old would have expressed just such a beauty as yours is now. So all their praises are but prophecies of this our time, prefiguring you ; and though they looked with eyes of divination, they still had not enough to sing your worth : while we in this present age have eyes to wonder, but lack the tongues to praise.

It is curious that commentators should not have noticed from this that Shakespeare was reading Chaucer, yet it is confirmed by the fact that he drew upon 'The Knight's Tale' for the plot of *A Midsummer Night's Dream* in this year 1593-4. Notice the consciousness of 'this our time' throughout the sestet, which carries forward to the famous sonnet following.

L. 12 : a number of editors have altered 'still' to 'skill' : there is no necessity. Though there is room for doubt, the change to 'skill' destroys the apposition, the contrasted sense, of the two last couplets.

107

Not mine own fears, nor the prophetic soul
Of the wide world dreaming on things to come,
Can yet the lease of my true love control,
Supposed as forfeit to a confined doom.
The mortal moon hath her eclipse endured,
And the sad augurs mock their own presage ;
Incertainties now crown themselves assured,
And peace proclaims olives of endless age.
Now with the drops of this most balmy time
My love looks fresh, and Death to me subscribes,
Since, spite of him, I'll live in this poor rhyme,
While he insults o'er dull and speechless tribes.
    And thou in this shalt find thy monument,
      When tyrants' crests and tombs of brass are spent.

Neither my own fears, nor the apprehensions of the world dwelling on what is to come, can yet determine the period of my love, supposed to be subject to mortality. The mortal moon has come through her eclipse, and the prophets of woe belie their own forecast ; uncertainties are now resolved, and the promise of permanent peace is proclaimed. Now with the dew of this balmy time my love looks fresh, and Death submits to me, since, in spite of him, I shall live in this verse, while he triumphs over dull, unlettered peoples. In this you shall find your monument when tyrants' crests and tombs of brass have crumbled away.

This sonnet rewards analysis, though all commentators have found its difficulties insurmountable. To the historian they are not ; their solution affords confirmatory evidence for the dating of the Sonnets. The convergence of the two historical events referred to in ll. 5-8 pinpoints the dating and makes it certain. To take ll. 7-8 first : these refer to the end of the long religious wars in France with the submission of Paris to Henri IV in March 1594 and the achievement of peace. In ll. 5-6 all Elizabethan scholars of any judgment recognise that 'the mortal moon' refers to Queen Elizabeth. She has come through an eclipse, a threat to her : as indeed she had this winter of 1593-4 with the Lopez conspiracy. Dr. Lopez, her personal physician, was found to be in touch with Spain with the idea of poisoning her, and he was executed in June 1594. These events made a great impression on Shakespeare's mind, as on other people's. The first contributed something to *Love's Labour's Lost* with the theme of Navarre's oath-breaking ; the second to *The Merchant of Venice* with its portrait of Shylock. We are then in the year 1594.

The amount of nonsense written about this famous sonnet, in the absence of precise dating, is astonishing.

108

What's in the brain that ink may character
Which hath not figured to thee my true spirit?
What's new to speak, what new to register,
That may express my love, or thy dear merit?
Nothing, sweet boy; but yet, like prayers divine,
I must each day say o'er the very same,
Counting no old thing old, thou mine, I thine,
Even as when first I hallowed thy fair name.
So that eternal love in love's fresh case
Weighs not the dust and injury of age,
Nor gives to necessary wrinkles place,
But makes antiquity for aye his page;
    Finding the first conceit of love there bred,
    Where time and outward form would show it dead.

108

What's in the brain that may be written down in ink which has not described to you my true spirit ? What is there new to say that may express my love or your worth ? Nothing, dear friend ; but yet, like divine service, I must every day say over the same, counting nothing outdated, you mine, I yours, just as when first I blessed your name. So that love, being eternally new, takes no account of the dust and injury of age, nor gives place to inevitable wrinkles, but makes even old age its servitor ; finding the first impression of love still there, where time and outward appearance would suppose it dead.

———————

Inspiration seems running short, and indeed what wonder ? Shakespeare admits as much in the octave, yet contrives to give the old theme a new turn in the sestet. Again he shows himself very self-conscious on the subject of 'wrinkles', several times mentioned already — perhaps understandably for an actor.

109

O, never say that I was false of heart,
Though absence seemed my flame to qualify :
As easy might I from myself depart
As from my soul, which in thy breast doth lie.
That is my home of love : if I have ranged,
Like him that travels, I return again ;
Just to the time, not with the time exchanged,
So that myself bring water for my stain.
Never believe, though in my nature reigned
All frailties that besiege all kinds of blood,
That it could so preposterously be stained
To leave for nothing all thy sum of good :
    For nothing this wide universe I call,
    Save thou, my rose ; in it thou art my all.

109

Do not say that I was false in heart, though absence seemed to make my love less warm — I might as easily depart from myself as from my soul, which lies in your breast. That is my love's home : if I have rangèd, like a traveller, I return home again : punctually to the time, not changing with the time, so that I myself bring water to wash away my stain. Though in my nature there reign all the frailties that besiege all kinds of blood, do not believe it could receive so preposterous a stain as to leave all your good for nothing : for I call the whole universe nothing without you, my rose ; in it you are all in all to me.

Very interesting autobiographically. It confirms that Shakespeare has been absent from Southampton, going about the country, and has been less attentive than of old in his offerings of duty. We detect a note of assured independence beneath the affection : with his share in the Lord Chamberlain's Company he now has security. In 1594 the theatres were active again, and it is clear from this and the next sonnet that Shakespeare was also on tour at some time this year. In these circumstances he may well have appeared to be neglectful ; but he returns from touring punctually to the time, l. 7. More interesting is the confession, ll. 9-10, of the frailties of his sportive blood, where he confirms the traditional stories and our knowledge of his ways with women. Nevertheless, he insists that his love is for Southampton alone, 'my rose'. No particular difficulties except perhaps for l. 7.

110

Alas, 'tis true I have gone here and there,
And made myself a motley to the view,
Gored mine own thoughts, sold cheap what is most dear,
Made old offences of affections new.
Most true it is that I have looked on truth
Askance and strangely ; but, by all above,
These blenches gave my heart another youth,
And worse essays proved thee my best of love.
Now all is done, have what shall have no end :
Mine appetite I never more will grind
On newer proof, to try an older friend,
A god in love, to whom I am confined.
   Then give me welcome, next my heaven the best,
   Even to thy pure and most most loving breast.

110

Alas, it is true that I have gone here and there and exposed myself as
a jester on the stage, wounded my inmost feelings, sold cheap what
is most dear, given offence to old affections by entertaining new
ones. It is true that I have looked askance at truth ; but these
digressions made me feel young again, and other experiences
proved you my best love. Now all that is over, accept what shall be
for good : I never more will whet my appetite on newer acquaintance, to try an older friend — a god in love to whom I am bound.
Then give me a welcome, next heaven the best I know, even to
your pure, loving heart.

———

Fascinating autobiographically : it shows us something of what Shakespeare had been up to while away on tour in the country in 1594, and what
he felt about it. Once more he lets us into the secret of his feelings about
his profession as an actor and confesses how much he minded making
himself a motley to the view, exposing his own feelings, selling cheap
what was most dear to him. In addition, he had been having other experiences in the realm of affection — which made him feel young again, but
made him reproach himself in coming back to Southampton. L. 7 : the
word 'blenches' means side-glances, a turning of the eye aside.

III

O, for my sake do you with Fortune chide,
The guilty goddess of my harmful deeds,
That did not better for my life provide
Than public means, which public manners breeds.
Thence comes it that my name receives a brand,
And almost thence my nature is subdued
To what it works in, like the dyer's hand :
Pity me then and wish I were renewed.
Whilst, like a willing patient, I will drink
Potions of eisel 'gainst my strong infection :
No bitterness that I will bitter think,
Nor double penance to correct correction.
    Pity me then, dear friend, and I assure ye
    Even that your pity is enough to cure me.

III

Chide Fortune for my sake — the goddess responsible for my ill deeds — that did not provide better for my life than a public profession, which breeds public manners. For with that is my name branded, and my nature almost subdued to what it works in, like the dyer's stained hand. Then pity me and wish I were made new again ; whilst, a willing patient, I will drink doses of vinegar against my strong infection. There is no medicine that I will think too bitter, nor refuse double penance to correct my failings. Pity me, dear friend, and I assure you that your pity even is enough to cure me.

––––––––

This carries the theme of the previous sonnet a stage further and takes us into the recesses of the gentlemanly Shakespeare's resentment against having to follow the profession that brought him his fame. Even his name, he thinks, 'receives a brand' therefrom, his nature almost 'subdued to what it works in'. L. 10 refers to the use of vinegar as a prophylactic against the plague.

112

Your love and pity doth the impression fill
Which vulgar scandal stamped upon my brow ;
For what care I who calls me well or ill,
So you o'er-green my bad, my good allow ?
You are my all the world, and I must strive
To know my shames and praises from your tongue :
None else to me, nor I to none alive,
That my steeled sense or changes right or wrong.
In so profound abysm I throw all care
Of others' voices, that my adder's sense
To critic and to flatterer stoppèd are.
Mark how with my neglect I do dispense :
   You are so strongly in my purpose bred
   That all the world besides methinks are dead.

112

Your love and pity erase the mark which vulgar scandal stamped upon my brow ; for what do I care who calls me well or ill so long as you cover my bad and approve what is good ? You are all the world to me, and I must strive to know my faults and good points from your tongue : there is no one else to me, nor do I take anyone in the world into account, that changes my fixed determination, whether right or wrong. Into so deep an abyss I throw all care of others' voices, that like the adder I stop my ears to critic and flatterer alike. Mark how I excuse my neglect of you : you are so strongly entrenched in my mind that I consider all the world besides as dead.

This sonnet is no less interesting from the literary point of view. It refers back to Greene's attack upon Shakespeare in 1592 as an upstart actor taking the place of the playwrights and stealing their feathers. We know how keenly Shakespeare felt this from Chettle's apology for letting the reflections upon him appear in print : 'because myself have seen his demeanour no less civil than he excellent in the quality he professes. Besides, divers of worship have reported his uprightness of dealing, which argues his honesty, and his facetious grace in writing, that approves his art.' (q. Chambers, vol. II, p. 189.) No doubt Southampton had been one of the worshipful persons to vouch for his uprightness of dealing. The use of the word 'o'er-green', l. 4, Shakespeare's own coinage, makes it fairly certain that this was 'the vulgar scandal' that had left its mark upon him. Still more interesting is Shakespeare's conclusion to pay no attention to 'others' voices', whether of critic or flatterer. How wise of him, especially to pay no attention to critics — or he might never have got his work done. It is nice to have here precisely what Shakespeare thought of them. Ll. 7-8 are difficult, for two sentences are telescoped together : I have extracted the sense.

113

Since I left you mine eye is in my mind,
And that which governs me to go about
Doth part his function and is partly blind,
Seems seeing, but effectually is out :
For it no form delivers to the heart
Of bird, of flower, or shape which it doth latch :
Of his quick object hath the mind no part,
Nor his own vision holds what it doth catch :
For if it see the rud'st or gentlest sight,
The most sweet favour or deformedest creature,
The mountain or the sea, the day or night,
The crow or dove, it shapes them to your feature.
 Incapable of more, replete with you,
 My most true mind thus maketh mine untrue.

113

Since I left you my eye is in my mind, and that which enables me to go about part performs its function and is part blind, seems to see but effectively is put out. For it presents to the mind no form of bird or flower, or shape that it grasps : the mind has no hold upon passing objects, nor does the vision retain what it perceives. Beholding the rudest or the gentlest sight, the most attractive or the most deformed appearance, mountain or sea, day or night, crow or dove, it shapes them to your likeness. Incapable of more, filled with the thought of you, the truest part of my mind makes me see things untruly.

Very much a duty-sonnet, rather artificial, written in absence ; we cannot but admire the ingenuity with which Shakespeare keeps the ball rolling. Beneath the protestations I think we can feel increasing independence from Southampton, an inevitable moving away in mind, however much his poet protests. The sonnet is not altogether easy, *e.g.* to catch the exact meaning of ll. 1-4. and l. 14. L. 1 has a parallel in *Lucrece*, l. 1426, 'save to the eye of mind'.

Or whether doth my mind, being crowned with you,
Drink up the monarch's plague, this flattery ?
Or whether shall I say mine eye saith true,
And that your love taught it this alchemy,
To make of monsters and things indigest
Such cherubins as your sweet self resemble,
Creating every bad a perfect best,
As fast as objects to his beams assemble ?
O, 'tis the first ; 'tis flattery in my seeing,
And my great mind most kingly drinks it up :
Mine eye well knows what with his gust is 'greeing,
And to his palate doth prepare the cup.
    If it be poisoned, 'tis the lesser sin
    That mine eye loves it and does first begin.

Rather far-fetched to our taste, and not really congenial to Shakespeare's.
Perhaps we see him not only struggling to say something new — difficult
enough in itself — but trying to respond to the increasingly metaphysical
strain among the younger poets, looking for more intellectual content in
verse than that which the early 1590s displayed. In l. 5, 'things indigest'
comes from a phrase of Ovid, that impressed itself upon Shakespeare's
mind from his schooldays : 'rudis indigestaque moles', which appears in
3 Henry VI, where Gloucester is described as 'an indigested and deformed
lump'. More interesting is Shakespeare's pointed reference to flattery as
'the monarch's plague'. This cannot be without some thought of the
Queen in mind. Shakespeare's affiliation to Southampton brought him
into proximity with the opposition attitude towards her, and it was
observed at the time of her death that Shakespeare offered no tribute of
verse in her memory. She had kept Southampton in the Tower during
the last two years of her life, for his part in the Essex conspiracy. But

114

Perhaps my mind, being crowned with you, drinks up flattery — the plague of monarchs ? Or shall I say that my eye tells true and that your love taught it this alchemy, to turn monsters and mis-shapen things into such cherubins as resemble you, creating out of every ill object a perfect best, as fast as things pass before my sight ? It is the first, rather — flattery in my seeing, and like a monarch my mind drinks it up : my eye knows quite well what appeals to it, and prepares the cup according to taste : if it is poisoned, it is the lesser sin that my eye loves it and leads the mind on.

———

already during the period of the Sonnets she was expressing her disappro-val of Southampton — for his virtual breach of promise to marry Burgh-ley's grand-daughter, for not taking up his family responsibilities, perhaps for his conduct in general. She must have known a thing or two.

Ll. 10-11 are fascinating psychologically. An early tradition tells us that Shakespeare played kingly parts. Once before, in Sonnet 87, we have seen him thinking of himself, in sleep, as a king. Who at this moment was flattering him ? I think it must refer to the very favourable reception of his two poems, each 'crowned with you', *i.e.* a dedication to Southampton.

115

Those lines that I before have writ do lie,
Even those that said I could not love you dearer ;
Yet then my judgment knew no reason why
My most full flame should afterwards burn clearer.
But reckoning Time, whose millioned accidents
Creep in 'twixt vows and change decrees of kings,
Tan sacred beauty, blunt the sharp'st intents,
Divert strong minds to the course of altering things :
Alas, why — fearing of Time's tyranny —
Might I not then say 'Now I love you best',
When I was certain o'er incertainty,
Crowning the present, doubting of the rest ?
    Love is a babe ; then might I not say so,
    To give full growth to that which still doth grow.

115

Those lines that I have written before lie — even those that said I could not love you dearer ; but then my judgment knew no reason why my full flame should burn more clearly afterwards. Only there was Time to take account of, whose innumerable accidents creep in between vows and change kings' decrees, darken beauty, blunt the keenest intentions, divert strong minds to different courses. Alas, fearing the tyranny of Time, why might I not say then, 'Now I love you best' — when after uncertainty I had achieved certainty, crowning the present, doubtful of everything else ? The answer is that love is a child : might I not say so, to allow for full growth to what is still growing.

———————

Also rather laboured ; and underneath the asseverations we cannot but feel that Shakespeare is moving away in mind. Still we learn something about the course of the relationship — that he had achieved certainty after a period of uncertainty. The crux of the somewhat strained argument is reached in the last couplet : why could I not, when I had achieved certainty, say 'Now I love you best ? ' Because love is as a child, whose full growth is to come, and my love still grows. At this point we may take leave to wonder.

116

Let me not to the marriage of true minds
Admit impediments : love is not love
Which alters when it alteration finds,
Or bends with the remover to remove.
O, no ! it is an ever-fixèd mark
That looks on tempests and is never shaken ;
It is the star to every wandering bark,
Whose worth's unknown, although his height be taken.
Love's not Time's fool, though rosy lips and cheeks
Within his bending sickle's compass come ;
Love alters not with his brief hours and weeks,
But bears it out even to the edge of doom :
  If this be error and upon me proved,
  I never writ, nor no man ever loved.

116

Let me not admit impediments to the marriage of true minds : love
is not love which alters when it meets with alteration, or changes
when one of them changes. No, it is a fixed beacon that looks on
storms and is not shaken ; it is the star to every voyaging ship, whose
value is not calculable although its altitude is. Love is not the sport
of Time, though rosy lips and cheeks come within the compass of
his sickle ; love does not alter with the days, but keeps straight on
to the threshold of doomsday. If this be error proved against me,
I never wrote and no man ever loved.

———

Shakespeare comes clear with this famous sonnet after the note of dubiety
and apology in the previous ones. All the same, in spite of its confession
of faith, or because of it, it sounds like a valediction. Ll. 1-2 reflect the
marriage-service in the Prayer Book.

117

Accuse me thus — that I have scanted all
Wherein I should your great deserts repay,
Forgot upon your dearest love to call,
Whereto all bonds do tie me day by day ;
That I have frequent been with unknown minds,
And given to time your own dear-purchased right ;
That I have hoisted sail to all the winds
Which should transport me farthest from your sight.
Book both my wilfulness and errors down,
And on just proof surmise accumulate ;
Bring me within the level of your frown,
But shoot not at me in your wakened hate :
   Since my appeal says I did strive to prove
   The constancy and virtue of your love.

You may charge me with neglecting the duty I have to requite your great deserts, forgetting to call upon your love, to which I am by all bonds daily bound ; with frequenting strangers, and giving to the world in general the right you purchased dearly ; with hoisting sail to all the winds that take me farthest from you. Put down both my wilfulness and my errors to my account, and add your suspicions to what is justly proved against me ; bring me within the compass of your disapproval, but do not shoot at me in your awakened dislike : since my appeal is that I was striving to test the constancy and trueness of your love.

This indicates something of a breach, and that Southampton had cause for resenting Shakespeare's conduct. It is not difficult to read between the lines that now that Shakespeare was secure, and in any case wholly taken up with his work for the Lord Chamberlain's Company both as actor and as playwright, he had not the time to give to his young patron that he had had in the years 1592 and 1593. New prospects were opening before him, new acquaintance which he would need to pursue and which took him away from Southampton. The young patron clearly resented this, since he had a 'dear-purchased right' to Shakespeare, on the score of both love and financial support. L. 4, I think, may refer to the obligation Shakespeare owed his patron for the purchase of a share in the Company, since it is described as tying him 'day by day' ; but he confesses that 'all bonds' tie him to his patron. L. 11 offers an interesting parallel with *A Lover's Complaint*, ll. 309-10, where Southampton was in mind as the attractive, but errant, young man :

> That not a hurt which in his level came
> Could scape the hail of his all-hurting aim.

L. 12, 'wakened hate' is very strong : there is something serious up between them.

118

Like as to make our appetites more keen
With eager compounds we our palate urge ;
As to prevent our maladies unseen
We sicken to shun sickness when we purge :
Even so, being full of your ne'er cloying sweetness,
To bitter sauces did I frame my feeding,
And sick of welfare found a kind of meetness
To be diseased, ere that there was true needing.
Thus policy in love, to anticipate
The ills that were not, grew to faults assured,
And brought to medicine a healthful state
Which, rank of goodness, would by ill be cured.
But thence I learn, and find the lesson true,
Drugs poison him that so fell sick of you.

To arouse our appetites we sharpen our palates with tart contrasts ; to forestall illness we make ourselves sick with medicine in purging. Even so, being full of your sweetness, though without cloying, I set myself to feed on bitter sauces ; and filled with well-being, I found a kind of meetness in being sick, before there was any need for it. Thus thinking to follow a policy in love, to anticipate ills not yet come, made for real faults and subjected to medicine a healthy state, which — too rich with goodness — would be cured by ill. But thence I learnt a true lesson — that such drugs poison him that in this way sickened of you.

What a curious sonnet, and yet how convincing psychologically ! In such a relationship the moment is apt to arrive when the palate is somewhat jaded and needs reviving. The friend (or lover) turns elsewhere, to new acquaintance, new experiences — not necessarily better : indeed Shakespeare does not much relish his choice or his experience :

> To bitter sauces did I frame my feeding.

But he wanted a change, and in this accepts responsibility for his deliberate action. The people whose company he sought were not in themselves very desirable — certainly not in comparison with Southampton. But there was a danger of this relationship cloying : one hears the apprehension beneath the assurance. One feels that when it comes to this, love is coming to an end.

Nevertheless, Shakespeare makes poetry out of it : he turns *everything* to account — it is one of his most salient characteristics from the beginning. And the sonnet, though hardly congenial, is ingenious : one is reminded of Swift's Stella quenching a too curious inquirer with 'It is well known that the Dean can write well upon a broomstick'.

Yet the sonnet is true, too, to the facts of Elizabethan life. For the horrors of purging, cf. my *Ralegh and the Throckmortons*, pp. 276-7, 295.

119

What potions have I drunk of Siren tears
Distilled from limbecks foul as hell within,
Applying fears to hopes and hopes to fears,
Still losing when I saw myself to win !
What wretched errors hath my heart committed,
Whilst it hath thought itself so blessèd never !
How have mine eyes out of their spheres been fitted
In the distraction of this madding fever !
O benefit of ill : now I find true
That better is by evil still made better,
And ruined love, when it is built anew,
Grows fairer than at first, more strong, far greater.
  So I return rebuked to my content,
  And gain by ills thrice more than I have spent.

What potions have I drunk of woman's tears — distilled from alembics as foul as hell within, applying fears to my hopes and raising my hopes when I am discouraged, for ever losing when I thought I was going to win ! What miserable errors has my heart committed, while it thought itself never so blessed ! How have my eyes been distracted in this mad fever ! But I have drawn this benefit from ill : now I find it true that good is bettered by evil, and ruined love, when renewed, grows fairer and stronger than at first. Thus chastened I return to what gives me content, and by the ills I have experienced gain greatly more than I have lost.

———

Here is the upshot ; here is not artifice, but sincerity. This sonnet makes the transition from the young man to Shakespeare's mistress, and, as we shall see, he comes to speak always of his infatuation for her as a fever, which he does not approve, but cannot help. The 'Siren tears' refers to his mistress ; the alembics 'foul as hell within' obviously not written for her eyes.

Shakespeare's ill experience — we shall see it corroborated in the sonnets dealing with his mistress — brought him back in mind to his friend. And that some good comes from ill is a very Shakespearean thought, constant throughout his work. The theme then is that of *redintegratio amoris*, of love renewed and made stronger for a breach. But — 'ruined love' — I wonder.

L. 14 : editors have followed Malone in altering the original 'ills' to 'ill'. There is no need for this ; indeed it weakens the concrete sense of Shakespeare's ill experiences with the mistress, and I have kept to the original.

120

That you were once unkind befriends me now,
And for that sorrow which I then did feel
Needs must I under my transgression bow,
Unless my nerves were brass or hammered steel.
For if you were by my unkindness shaken
As I by yours, you've passed a hell of time ;
And I, a tyrant, have no leisure taken
To weigh how once I suffered in your crime.
O, that our night of woe might have remembered
My deepest sense, how hard true sorrow hits,
And soon to you, as you to me then, tendered
The humble salve which wounded bosoms fits !
    But that your trespass now becomes a fee :
    Mine ransoms yours, and yours must ransom me.

120

The fact that you were once unkind is a help to me now, and, as against the suffering which I felt then, I must needs be bent by my transgression, unless my nerves are of brass or steel. For if you were shaken by my unkindness as I was by yours, you've been through hell ; and I, like a tyrant, have not taken the trouble to think how it was when I suffered at your hand. O, that our night of suffering might have recalled me to my deepest sense — how hard true sorrow hits, and that I had tendered to you, as you did to me, the comfort that befits wounded breasts ! But your trespass now becomes something in recompense : mine ransoms yours, as yours must mine.

———

Both Shakespeare and Southampton have been in the wrong against each other, Shakespeare now as his young friend earlier. It is clear that Shakespeare has been neglecting his patron, to whom he owed so much, for the woman in question. We do not know which 'trespass' of Southampton's Shakespeare is here referring to : it may be either his affair with the mistress, or his defection to Marlowe, or both. In spite of Shakespeare's being in the wrong, one has the sense of his feeling of independence, of security, equality, as never in the earlier sonnets.

It is interesting to observe the religious language of the poem — 'transgression', 'trespass', 'ransom' : all of them words that Shakespeare was familiar with from early days in church.

121

'Tis better to be vile than vile esteemed,
When not to be receives reproach of being ;
And the just pleasure lost, which is so deemed
Not by our feeling, but by others' seeing.
For why should others' false adulterate eyes
Give salutation to my sportive blood ?
Or on my frailties why are frailer spies,
Which in their wills count bad what I think good ?
No, I am that I am, and they that level
At my abuses reckon up their own :
I may be straight, though they themselves be bevel,
By their rank thoughts my deeds must not be shown :
    Unless this general evil they maintain —
    All men are bad, and in their badness reign.

121

It is better to be bad than to be thought so, when, if one is not, one has the reproach of being so : there is one's just pleasure lost, condemned not by our own feeling but by other people's opinions. For, why should others' adulterous eyes take note of my wanton ways ? Or those even frailer than I spy on my frailties, deliberately putting down as bad what I think good ? No, I am what I am, and they that make my ill doings their target expose their own : I may be straight, and they themselves may be crooked, my deeds must not be judged by their ill thoughts — unless they hold it as a general view that all men are bad and bent on evil ways.

Of crucial importance autobiographically, for in it Shakespeare tells us what he thinks of himself morally. With absolute honesty he does not hold himself in high esteem. He knows himself too well ; but he also knows other people too well to submit himself, or his pleasures, or his 'sportive blood', to their judgment. Why live our lives in the light of other people's eyes ? He calls theirs 'false adulterate eyes', and regrets any just pleasure lost for their condemnation, not from any real feeling of our own.

There follows the magnificent, quasi-Biblical, affirmation, 'I am that I am', which commands our respect in one with such knowledge of himself — as we have seen, never any excuses, always ready to accept more than his share of responsibility. There is a parallel in *3 Henry VI*, V. vi. 83 : 'I am myself alone'.

L. 11 : the word 'bevel' means sloping, at an angle. No other difficulty, but nearly all the commentators have been bedevilled by humbug over this sonnet and refusing to look it in the face. It is about the notorious affair with the dark lady.

122

Thy gift, thy tables, are within my brain
Full charactered with lasting memory,
Which shall above that idle rank remain
Beyond all date even to eternity.
Or, at the least, so long as brain and heart
Have faculty by nature to subsist,
Till each to razed oblivion yield his part
Of thee, thy record never can be missed.
That poor retention could not so much hold,
Nor need I tallies thy dear love to score,
Therefore to give them from me was I bold,
To trust those tables that receive thee more :
    To keep an adjunct to remember thee
    Were to import forgetfulness in me.

Your gift, your jottings, are registered lastingly in my brain — to remain beyond the rank of mere memoranda in a book, even for ever. Or, at least, so long as brain and heart subsist, till each yields up its part of you to oblivion erasing all things, your record will never be wanting. That poor container of a book could not hold so much, nor do I need tallies with which to score up your love : therefore was I so bold as to give your notebook away, to trust those tablets of memory that have more of you. To keep an external aid to remember you would imply forgetfulness in me.

———

Southampton had given Shakespeare a notebook, perhaps with some notes of his own, and Shakespeare has given it away. It seems a curious thing to have done and to need explanation. But Shakespeare is never at a loss, and explains it away : Southampton is so engraved on his memory that he does not need a memoranda-book to remember him by. Ingenious as ever — but the action has the flavour of the end of love to me. The explanation, however, made another subject for a sonnet, when subjects for variation were running short.

The suggestion seems to derive from Ronsard :

> Il ne falloit, Maîtresse, autres tablettes
> Pour vous graver que celles de mon cœur,
> Où de sa main Amour, notre vainqueur,
> Vous a gravée, et vos grâces parfaites.

Perhaps, therefore, Shakespeare's action was notional, to provide a sonnet : it would otherwise be uncharacteristic of him.

123

No, Time, thou shalt not boast that I do change ;
Thy pyramids built up with newer might
To me are nothing novel, nothing strange :
They are but dressings of a former sight.
Our dates are brief, and therefore we admire
What thou dost foist upon us that is old,
And rather make them born to our desire
Than think that we before have heard them told.
Thy registers and thee I both defy,
Not wondering at the present nor the past,
For thy records and what we see doth lie
Made more or less by thy continual haste :
    This I do vow and this shall ever be,
    I will be true despite thy scythe and thee.

123

Time, you shall not boast that I change ; the pyramids you pile up
ever more powerfully are not at all novel or strange to me : they
are but elaborations of what has been seen before. Our lives are
brief, and therefore we wonder more at things you foist upon us
from the past, and rather conceive them shaped to our desire than
think them what we have heard of before. I defy both your records
and you, wondering neither at the present nor the past, for your
evidences and what we see both lie, waxing and waning with your
hurried course. This I vow, as it shall ever be : I will be true, despite you and your fell scythe.

———

At first sight it seems that inspiration is running out and that Shakespeare
is repeating himself. Ideas and phrases are here from earlier sonnets, yet
all the same he gives the theme of time a new twist, even if it is difficult
to grasp the not very precise argument. The 'pyramids' in l. 2 have
usually been interpreted metaphorically, as all that Time piles up. But I
rather think that Shakespeare's mind, concrete and visual, had the fan-
tastic buildings of the age in view — such skyscrapers as Wollaton,
Holdenby, Kenilworth, Nonsuch. His preference for what was old is
very characteristic of the man, so much of whose inspiration came from
the past.

124

If my dear love were but the child of state,
It might for fortune's bastard be unfathered
As subject to time's love or to time's hate,
Weeds among weeds, or flowers with flowers gathered.
No, it was builded far from accident ;
It suffers not in smiling pomp, nor falls
Under the blow of thrallèd discontent
Whereto the inviting time our fashion calls :
It fears not policy, that heretic,
Which works on leases of short-numbered hours,
But all alone stands hugely politic,
That it nor grows with heat nor drowns with showers.
 To this I witness call the fools of time,
 Which die for goodness who have lived for crime.

If my love were merely politic it might be discountenanced when fortune turned unfavourable — as dependent on time's love and so gathered with the flowers, or on time's hate and so plucked up as a weed. But no : it was not built upon chance circumstance ; it is not affected by prosperity, nor does it fall under the blows with which discontent is kept down, and in which the time is prone to set a fashion. It is not prudential — a heresy in love — to operate on leases of a few short hours, but stands up on its own in monumental state, affected neither by fair weather nor foul. In witness I call those dupes of time, who die as martyrs, but are guilty of crime against the state.

———

This difficult sonnet is fascinating from every point of view, personal and autobiographical, historical and chronological. But it is extremely rewarding to work it out and get it right. Hyder Rollins tells us, in the *New Variorum* edition of the Sonnets, vol. I. pp. 311-12, that 'extraordinarily numerous and divergent are the historical references that have been detected in these fourteen lines. None has been or can be proved.' The mass of commentary on this sonnet has been more than usually pointless ; for it is completely explicable to anyone who knows the circumstances of the time.

In the first place, all can see that the poem is politico-religious in its references : 'thrallèd discontent', 'policy', 'heretic', 'politic', 'crime', 'child of state'. In the second, it is completely corroborative of our time-scheme, consistent with the chronology we have seen unfolded. In 1594-5 the government's campaign against the Jesuits reached its culmination with the execution of a larger number than at any time for the rest of the reign. Among these were such well-known Jesuits as Robert Southwell and Henry Walpole, or, among lesser known, Father John Cornelius with whose case Ralegh was connected. The Parliament of 1593 had passed two statutes tightening up the laws against Catholic recusants, for retaining the Queen's subjects in obedience, and against seminary priests reconciling her subjects to Rome. The second Act, 35 Eliz. Cap. 11, refers to the 'wicked and seditious persons who, terming themselves Catholics and being indeed spies and intelligencers not only for her Majesty's foreign enemies but also for rebellious and traitorous subjects born within her Highness's dominions, and hiding their most detestable and devilish purposes under a false pretext of religion and conscience ...' There, by the way, is the very point of the sonnet's last line: 'the fools of time, which die for goodness who have lived for crime'. They died as martyrs for religion, but the Elizabethan government's view was that the Jesuits in particular, involved as some of them were in conspiracies against the state, constituted a fifth column in wartime. We find Shakespeare reflecting the ordinary point of view of people in general in this matter: he thought such martyrs 'the fools of time'.

But the situation under the surface is more complicated. For Southampton was a Catholic, though a politically respectable one, received at Court and not involved at this time in any treasonable activities. But he was not regarded with favour by the Queen or Burghley, and it was on his coming of age in 1594 that he was made to pay — according to the Jesuit, Henry Garnet — an immense sum for refusing to marry Burghley's grand-daughter.

So Southampton was at this time under the blows of fortune — this is the current of thought at the back of the sonnet; it reminds Southampton that Shakespeare's love was not founded on chance and was not subject to the ups and downs of fortune. It is so like his prudent mind — for it was in fact prudential — to write so indirectly about 'the blow of thrallèd discontent whereto the inviting time our fashion calls' and to be no more dangerously specific.

Nevertheless, the Sonnets — and perhaps the closeness of the relationship — were shortly to end.

125

Were't aught to me I bore the canopy,
With my extern the outward honouring,
Or laid great bases for eternity,
Which prove more short than waste or ruining ?
Have I not seen dwellers on form and favour
Lose all and more by paying too much rent
For compound sweet ; foregoing simple savour,
Pitiful thrivers in their gazing spent ?
No, let me be obsequious in thy heart,
And take thou my oblation, poor but free,
Which is not mixed with seconds, knows no art
But mutual render, only me for thee.
   Hence, thou suborned informer ! a true soul
   When most impeached stands least in thy control.

Were it anything to me that I bore the canopy over you, with my exterior honouring the outward man ; or laid foundations for eternity, which prove more brief than letting run to waste or go to ruin ? Have I not seen those who hang upon appearances lose all by paying too much for complex expectations, forgoing simple tastes — poor thrivers, utterly spent out in hopes ? No, let my devotion be of the heart : take my offering, poor but free, which is not mixed with chaff and knows no art but mutual exchange, only me for you. Away with those thoughts ! a true soul when most maligned with them is least under their influence.

———

This last sonnet in the Southampton sequence is most complex and suggestive, of a philosophical cast of reflexion, appropriate to the conclusion of so strange and momentous a relationship. Again, as so characteristically with Shakespeare, there is a suggestive secondary stratum going on under the surface-consciousness, that betrays itself in the imagery. (No man in the history of literature ever bore more completely the character, the stigmata, of the poet. The very words connect as if under water.) In l. 1, the word 'canopy' suggests the person of honour to whom all the sonnets have been written —

To one, of one, still such, and ever so.

The theme of the first quatrain is that the external honouring of his young lord meant little to Shakespeare — he had seen too much of life to attach importance to that brief pleasure. The second quatrain reflects on such persons as he had observed, hangers-on of the great, foregoing simple satisfactions for doubtful expectations, throwing away all they have on their hopes — pitiful thrivers, thriving not at all.

The third quatrain gives us Shakespeare's final statement of his own case : his offering to Southampton is 'poor but free', and it is again psychologically revealing that just at the moment of this affirmation his mind goes back to his country origins : his oblation is not 'mixed with seconds', *i.e.* the second-class flour after the best has been used. And he can conceive of the relationship only on a basis of mutual exchange and equality, 'only me for thee'.

In the last couplet, 'thou suborned informer' carries on the imagery from the previous sonnet — from the paid informers who spied on the Catholics and betrayed them. Here it is only an apostrophe to the imaginary source of the base thoughts in the first quatrain, to which the last couplet returns. There may, however, be a suggestion of reproach in the couplet, that Shakespeare felt maligned ('impeached') of just such thoughts as those by Southampton. They would be a natural enough, indeed an obvious, suspicion in such a relationship ; it would indeed be a very remarkable man who was wholly innocent of them. The reply is also obvious — that it is just when one is most suspected of such considerations that one is least influenced by them.

It may be so.

It is with this sonnet that the most extraordinary sequence in literature properly ends. And with no less propriety : we have come full circle from the deference and dependence of the early sonnets to the complete independence and assertion of equality of this. 'Poor but free' — after the submission to the young lord, the humility and tact, there is a lordliness on Shakespeare's part that comes through at the end.

126

O thou, my lovely boy, who in thy power
Dost hold Time's fickle glass, his sickle, hour :
Who hast by waning grown, and therein show'st
Thy lovers withering as thy sweet self grow'st :
If Nature, sovereign mistress over wrack,
As thou goest onwards still will pluck thee back,
She keeps thee to this purpose that her skill
May time disgrace and wretched minutes kill.
Yet fear her, O thou minion of her pleasure :
She may detain, but not still keep, her treasure !
Her audit, though delayed, answered must be,
And her quietus is to render thee.

126

O you, my lovely boy, who hold in your power Time's hour-glass and his sickle — you who wane as you grow older and in that show your friends withering as you yourself grow up : if Nature, sovereign mistress over chaos, as you go onwards will ever pluck you back, she keeps you to demonstrate her power to hold up time. Yet fear her, you who are Nature's darling : she may detain her treasure, but not keep it for ever. Her last account, though delayed, must be paid and her discharge is to render you up.

This poem of twelve lines in rhymed couplets may be taken to mark the end of the Southampton sonnet-sequence. Turning it into prose brings out, more clearly, if anything, that it is of the nature of an *envoi* : it sums up what may be regarded as the dominant theme, Time and its ineluctable destruction of beauty, and, by implication, of human relationships. True enough, only in Shakespeare's Sonnets does Southampton survive.

The commentators have made a great hash of ll. 3-4 : not one has been able to take Shakespeare's phrase, 'who has by waning grown', directly and simply, meaning that the young man's beauty wanes as he grows older. Yet this is no very esoteric idea — perhaps the whole experience of the Sonnets is so remote from anything that has come their way or that they could possibly understand. The meaning of ll. 3-4 becomes simple and straightforward, and not in contrast or apposition : as the youth's beauty wanes, so his friends wither as he grows older. (The idea suggests, however, a further reverberation.) Shakespeare's concern with the ebb and flow of things, their waxing and waning, their growing by waning, and renewing by wasting, is very Ovidian : the chief school influence that remained with him all his life.

L. 5 : the use of the word 'wrack' is paralleled in both *Venus and Adonis*, l. 558, and *Lucrece*, ll. 841, 966. In the last line the word 'quietus' comes from the old Latin inscription on an account, *quietus est* =he is quit.

127

In the old age black was not counted fair,
Or if it were it bore not beauty's name ;
But now is black beauty's successive heir,
And beauty slandered with a bastard shame :
For since each hand hath put on nature's power,
Fairing the foul with art's false borrowed face,
Sweet beauty hath no name, no holy bower,
But is profaned, if not lives in disgrace.
Therefore my mistress' eyes are raven black,
Her eyes so suited, and they mourners seem
As such who, not born fair, no beauty lack,
Slandering creation with a false esteem :
    Yet so they mourn, becoming of their woe,
    That every tongue says beauty should look so.

We have to think of Sonnets 1-126 as a continuous sequence, in an intelligible order ; and I think the remaining sonnets, in which Shakespeare's relationship with his mistress is the dominant theme, are so too : they unfold a developing story. But, in time, they interpose themselves into the midst of the Southampton sequence — naturally, for their story is mixed up with his in the triangular relationship that came to be formed.

This sonnet, with its emphasis on women's painting, recalls Sonnet 67, and is closely paralleled by *Love's Labour's Lost*, IV. iii. 249 foll., where Berowne, who expresses Shakespeare's point of view, says :

No face is fair that is not full so black . . .
O, if in black my lady's brows be decked,
It mourns that painting and usurping hair
Should ravish doters with a false aspect ;
And therefore is she born to make black fair.
Her favour turns the fashion of the days,
For native blood is counted painting now ;
And therefore red, that would avoid dispraise,
Paints itself black to imitate her brow.

127

In former times black was not accounted fair, or, if it were, it was not called beautiful; but now black is the proper heir to beauty, and beauty itself is slandered as artificial. For since every hand has assumed nature's power, making foul into fair with borrowed art, beauty herself has no name or refuge sacred to her, but is profaned, if not disgraced. So it is that my mistress's eyes are raven-black, as is her hair, and they seem to mourn that those who possess beauty, though not born fair, slander creation by being held in false esteem. Yet they mourn so becomingly that every tongue says beauty should look like that.

Love's Labour's Lost was written in 1593, which gives us a dating for this sonnet and helps us with its argument.

This artificial poem is curiously difficult to interpret, in its general argument no less than in detailed phrasing. It reminds us that formerly in Elizabethan days black was not counted beautiful, in women's hair, eyes, etc. But now since the rise of painting it is difficult to tell, dark is turned into fair by artificial means: so beauty is not herself, is profaned and driven into retreat. Therefore Shakespeare affirms that his mistress has dark eyes and hair, her eyes seeming to mourn that being beautiful, though not fair, the admiration her beauty attracts is thought misplaced.

L. 10, 'her eyes so suited': no commentator seems to have hit on the sense of that. Yet one should always remember Shakespeare's visual imagination: the meaning is literal and refers to the suit of black around her eyes — eyelashes, brows, hair all black: like Berowne's Rosaline in *Love's Labour's Lost*, who was evidently inspired by the dark mistress of the Sonnets.

128

How oft when thou, my music, music play'st
Upon that blessèd wood whose motion sounds
With thy sweet fingers, when thou gently sway'st
The wiry concord that mine ear confounds,
Do I envy those jacks that nimble leap
To kiss the tender inward of thy hand ;
Whilst my poor lips, which should that harvest reap,
At the wood's boldness by thee blushing stand.
To be so tickled they would change their state
And situation with those dancing chips,
O'er whom thy fingers walk with gentle gait,
Making dead wood more blest than living lips.
   Since saucy jacks so happy are in this,
   Give them thy fingers, me thy lips to kiss.

128

How often when you, my music, play music upon that lucky wood whose movement resounds to your fingers, when you gently sway the stringed concord that subdues my ear, I envy those keys that leap up nimbly to kiss your hand's tender palm — while my poor lips, which should be reaping that harvest, stand by you blushing at the wood's boldness. To be so tickled they would like to change place with those dancing chips, over whom your fingers walk so gently, making dead wood more fortunate than living mouth. Since mere saucy keys are so happy, give them your fingers and me your lips to kiss.

———

What a pretty picture this conjures up of the poet standing politely, but hopefully, beside the lady at the virginals — for the dark lady is evidently musical. It is interesting to compare this sonnet with that written on music to Southampton, Sonnet 8 :

> Music to hear, why hear'st thou music sadly ?
> Sweets with sweets war not, joy delights in joy :
> Why lov'st thou that which thou receiv'st not gladly,
> Or else receiv'st with pleasure thine annoy ?

One cannot but note the contrast in feeling between the one and the other. Though both the lady and the young man are addressed as music — 'my music', 'music to hear' — one observes how appropriate the sentiment of one is for a woman, the other for a young man. We may take our choice as to which, we feel, is the more affecting, the more resonant with feeling. We must remind ourselves that these sonnets, though concerned with the lady, came to Southampton : they were the productions of *his* poet.

The expense of spirit in a waste of shame
Is lust in action ; and till action, lust
Is perjured, murderous, bloody, full of blame,
Savage, extreme, rude, cruel, not to trust ;
Enjoyèd no sooner but despisèd straight,
Past reason hunted, and no sooner had
Past reason hated, as a swallowed bait
On purpose laid to make the taker mad,
Mad in pursuit and in possession so,
Had, having, and in quest to have, extreme ;
A bliss in proof, and proved, a very woe,
Before, a joy proposed, behind, a dream.
    All this the world well knows, yet none knows well
    To shun the heaven that leads men to this hell.

This virtuoso piece was probably suggested by Philip Sidney's sonnet on the same subject. Sidney is rather less explicit, and in consequence less powerful :

    Thou blind man's mark, thou fool's self-chosen snare,
    Fond fancy's scum, and dregs of scattered thought,
    Band of all evils, cradle of causeless care,
    Thou web of will, whose end is never wrought.

For people hardly realise the full subtlety in Shakespeare, that such a sonnet as this — always taken straight and rather heavily — is, in a sense, in inverted commas. It is a literary exercise, but it is also experience ; rather sudden, Shakespeare lost no time in getting down to business — in keeping with the traditional story of Shakespeare forestalling Burbage over an assignation made at the theatre : 'William the Conqueror was before Richard III.' We may imagine the pleasure such a poem gave Southampton and the young men among whom it was handed about.

129

Lust in action is the spilling of spirit in a waste of shame ; and till action, lust is perjured and cruel, bloody and savage, extreme, guilty, not to be trusted ; no sooner enjoyed than despised, past reason hunted, and no sooner had than past reason hated, as a swallowed bait laid on purpose to make a man mad, both in pursuit and in possession ; had, having, and seeking to have, without bounds ; the act itself bliss, as soon as over, regretted ; before, a joy proposed, afterwards, a dream. All this the world very well knows, yet no one knows how to avoid the heaven that leads men to this hell.

It is more illuminating to compare it with *Lucrece*, ll. 211 foll., Tarquin's reflection :

> What win I if I gain the thing I seek ?
> A dream, a breath, a froth of fleeting joy.
> Who buys a minute's mirth to wail a week,
> Or sells eternity to get a toy ?
> For one sweet grape who will the vine destroy ?

Lucrece was written 1593–4, the date of the affair with the Dark Lady. It was the dark side of that experience that entered into the poem, with its perturbed and gloomy atmosphere, its moral self-questionings and self-reproach, and marks it off from the gaiety and insouciance of *Venus and Adonis* of the previous year. L. 14, 'hell' has a secondary bawdy meaning, cf. Sonnet 144, l. 12.

130

My mistress' eyes are nothing like the sun,
Coral is far more red than her lips' red ;
If snow be white, why then her breasts are dun,
If hairs be wires, black wires grow on her head.
I have seen roses damasked, red and white,
But no such roses see I in her cheeks ;
And in some perfumes is there more delight
Than in the breath that from my mistress reeks.
I love to hear her speak, yet well I know
That music hath a far more pleasing sound ;
I grant I never saw a goddess go :
My mistress, when she walks, treads on the ground.
    And yet, by heaven, I think my love as rare
    As any she belied by false compare.

130

My mistress's eyes are not at all like the sun ; coral is of a far better red than her lips ; if snow is white, then her breasts are certainly not snow-white ; if hairs are to be thought of as wires, hers are not golden wires but black. I have seen damask-roses, mingled red and white, but I do not see such roses in her cheeks ; some perfumes give more delight than the breath that comes from her. I love to hear her speak, yet I know quite well that music sounds far better ; I never saw a goddess walk, I grant, but when my mistress walks she treads on the ground. And yet I think my love as rare as any woman belied by false comparisons.

————

This is even more of a literary exercise, and must have given more pure amusement to Southampton and his friends. For the poem can hardly have been presented to the dark lady, even as a joke. It is a skit on the unreal comparisons, the unconvincing deifications of their mistresses regular with the poets of the sonnet-sequences. In these the women are all goddesses, and nearly all the poets, even Spenser, refer to their hair as golden wires : the new art of head-tiring with wire, the curling and frizzing, made this a fashionable comparison. Shakespeare pokes fun at all these improbable comparisons : his mistress is not a goddess but a real woman, and she treads — do not forget the secondary suggestion — on the ground. And we learn definitely that her hair was black, which some commentators have doubted.

131

Thou art as tyrannous, so as thou art,
As those whose beauties proudly make them cruel ;
For well thou know'st to my dear dóting heart
Thou art the fairest and most precious jewel.
Yet, in good faith, some say that thee behold
Thy face hath not the power to make love groan :
To say they err I dare not be so bold,
Although I swear it to myself alone.
And to be sure that is not false I swear,
A thousand groans but thinking on thy face,
One on another's neck, do witness bear
Thy black is fairest in my judgment's place.
   In nothing art thou black save in thy deeds,
    And thence this slander, as I think, proceeds.

131

You are as tyrannical, even as you are, as those whose beauties make them cruel through pride ; for you know well that to my doting heart you are the fairest, most precious jewel. Yet, in good faith, some people beholding you say that your face has not the power to make love sigh : I dare not be so bold as to say they err, although I swear it to myself. And to be sure that what I swear is not false, a thousand sighs one upon another, when I but think on your face, bear witness that your black is fairest in my judgment. You are black in nothing save in your deeds — whence this slander takes its rise.

This sonnet brings us nearer to sincerity and the real situation. In fact, there is nothing in the whole sonnet-literature like the realism of Shakespeare's portrait of this woman. No illusion about himself or her. Now that we know who and what she was, we are not surprised to learn that her deeds too were 'black' ; yet Shakespeare is under her spell : to him her 'black is fairest'.

132

Thine eyes I love, and they, as pitying me,
Knowing thy heart torments me with disdain,
Have put on black and loving mourners be,
Looking with pretty ruth upon my pain.
And truly not the morning sun of heaven
Better becomes the grey cheeks of the east,
Nor that full star that ushers in the even
Doth half that glory to the sober west
As those two mourning eyes become thy face.
O, let it then as well beseem thy heart
To mourn for me, since mourning doth thee grace,
And suit thy pity like in every part.
  Then will I swear beauty herself is black,
  And all they foul that thy complexion lack.

132

I love your eyes and they, out of pity for me, knowing your heart disdains me, have put on black and look on me as mourners, showing a pretty compassion for my pain. And truly the morning sun does not better become the grey cheeks of dawn, nor does the star of evening do half that glory to the sober west as those two mourning eyes become your face. O, let it then as well befit your heart to mourn for me, since mourning graces you so well, and wear your pity alike in every part. Then I will swear beauty itself is black, and all that are not of your complexion foul.

Artificial as this is, it represents a further step in Shakespeare's infatuation. The lady is not in love with him, but her beautiful black eyes, which have the appearance of mourning, seem to take pity on him. It is a pretty comment that the moment Shakespeare is in love, he contradicts the sentiments of Sonnet 130 against false comparisons, for here the lady is compared to the morning sun and the evening star. We may take it as confirmation that he *is* in love. A pun on 'mourning' and 'morning', of course, runs all through the sonnet. It is amusing to observe similar verbal tricks that were doing duty for Southampton in the earlier sonnets turned with equal facility and ingenuity *à propos* of the lady.

133

Beshrew that heart that makes my heart to groan
For that deep wound it gives my friend and me !
Is't not enough to torture me alone
But slave to slavery my sweet'st friend must be ?
Me from myself thy cruel eye hath taken,
And my next self thou harder hast engrossed :
Of him, myself, and thee I am forsaken,
A torment thrice threefold thus to be crossed.
Prison my heart in thy steel bosom's ward,
But then my friend's heart let my poor heart bail ;
Whoe'er keeps me, let my heart be his guard,
Thou canst not then use rigour in my gaol.
　　And yet thou wilt, for I, being pent in thee,
　　Perforce am thine and all that is in me.

133

Curse that heart that makes my heart groan for the deep wound it gives my friend and me ! Is it not enough to torture me, without enslaving my dearest friend ? Your cruel eye has taken me from myself and engrossed my other self even more : I am deprived of him, myself, and you — a thrice threefold torment thus to be thwarted. Imprison my heart in your breast of steel, but then let my poor heart bail out my friend's ; whoever has me in durance, let my heart keep him : you cannot then make my imprisonment harsh. And yet you will, for I, being pent up in you, am yours perforce and all that is within me.

———

The sincerity deepens with the situation, for the mistress has got hold of the young man, 'engrosses' him — a course of action she does not choose to employ with Shakespeare : Southampton is a far better catch. We are back at the situation described in Sonnets 34 and 35 in relation to the young man. Here we have Shakespeare's view of it in relation to his mistress. We observe, with some little cynicism, that the mourning eyes, the 'loving mourners', etc. of the previous sonnets have become 'thy cruel eye'. No commentator seems to have unravelled the meaning of l. 11 :

    Whoe'er keeps me, let my heart be his guard.

But surely it is to be taken simply and literally ? — guard meant guard-house, *i.e.* let my heart keep him. Nor are the last three lines easy : what is meant is — if I may keep him, then my imprisonment may not be rigorous. Yet it will be, for since I am pent up in you, so is all that is in me, *i.e.* my friend too.

134

So, now I have confessed that he is thine
And I myself am mortgaged to thy will,
Myself I'll forfeit, so that other mine
Thou wilt restore to be my comfort still.
But thou wilt not, nor he will not be free,
For thou art covetous and he is kind ;
He learned but surety-like to write for me,
Under that bond that him as fast doth bind.
The statute of thy beauty thou wilt take,
Thou usurer that put'st forth all to use,
And sue a friend 'came debtor for my sake :
So him I lose through my unkind abuse.
　　Him have I lost ; thou hast both him and me ;
　　He pays the whole, and yet am I not free.

134

Now that I have confessed he is yours and I am myself mortgaged to your will, I am ready to forfeit myself if only you will restore that other mine to be my comfort. But you will not do so, nor will he be free, for you are covetous and he is kind. He learned but as security for me to write on my behalf, and under that obligation is now bound as fast himself. You will take advantage of your beauty, since you are a usurer putting all to use, and sue a friend who engaged himself for my sake ; so I lose him through my abuse of him. I have lost him ; you have both him and me ; he pays the whole debt, and yet I am not quit.

———

This adds something important to the story of the relations of the three. We learn that to advance his suit with the lady, Shakespeare had got his young friend to write on his behalf, and this was how Southampton had become entangled. He was now in fast ; the lady would naturally prefer such a choice morsel to the poet, so that Shakespeare has (temporarily) lost them both. L. 2 : we are introduced to the double suggestion of the word 'will', which plays such a part in these sonnets, meaning not only desire but sex. L. 11 is elliptical for 'And sue a friend who became debtor for my sake'.

135

Whoever hath her wish, thou hast thy will,
And Will to boot, and Will in overplus:
More than enough am I that vex thee still,
To thy sweet will making addition thus.
Wilt thou, whose will is large and spacious,
Not once vouchsafe to hide my will in thine ?
Shall will in others seem right gracious
And in my will no fair acceptance shine ?
The sea, all water, yet receives rain still
And in abundance addeth to his store :
So thou, being rich in will, add to thy will
One will of mine, to make thy large will more.
   Let no unkind, no fair beseechers kill :
   Think all but one, and me in that one will.

135

Whoever has her wish, you have your will, and Will at need, and Will in overplus : for I am more than enough in plaguing you, thus adding one more to your sweet will. Won't you, whose will is large and spacious, condescend once to hide my will in yours ? Shall will in others seem very acceptable and mine gain no acceptance ? The sea, all water, goes on receiving rain and adds to its store in abundance : so you, being very receptive, add to yours one will of mine, to make your large will more. Let no fair suitors be unkindly refused : think them all one and include me in that one will.

––––––

Now that we know the facts behind the Sonnets and the sense in which the Elizabethans used the word 'will', this sonnet — never hitherto interpreted — becomes completely clear. The difficulty lay in the first two lines, which now can be seen to mean : the lady has her sex, her husband, Will Lanier, and Will Shakespeare in addition. This sonnet, which has given the commentators pages of embarrassed headache, must have given much amusement to Shakespeare's young friends, and perhaps to the 'lady' too.

There was an Elizabethan phrase, 'a woman will have her will', which the sonnet plays upon.

136

If thy soul check thee that I come so near,
Swear to thy blind soul that I was thy Will,
And Will, thy soul knows, is admitted there :
Thus far for love, my love-suit, sweet, fulfil.
Will will fulfil the treasure of thy love,
Ay, fill it full with wills, and my will one.
In things of great receipt with ease we prove
Among a number one is reckoned none.
Then in the number let me pass untold,
Though in thy store's account I one must be ;
For nothing hold me, so it please thee hold
That nothing me, a something sweet to thee.
    Make but my name thy love, and love that still,
    And then thou lovest me, for my name is Will.

136

If your conscience upbraids you that I come so near, bid it shut its eyes and say that I was your Will ; for Will in conscience, is admitted there : thus far for love, fulfil my love-suit. Will will fulfil your love's treasure — certainly, fill it full with wills, so long as mine is one. In things of great capacity we easily prove that one hardly counts among a number. Then let me pass uncounted among the number, though I must be one in your reckoning ; hold me for a little thing so that it please you to hold that little me, a something sweet for you. Make but my name your love and continue to cherish it, and then you love me, for my name is Will.

———

We can now interpret l. 3 : it refers to the lady's husband, who — her soul knows — is properly admitted there. (The others improperly, of course.) The meaning is not at all difficult to follow, once the veil of humbug is removed from the eyes. The Victorians, however, kept it steadily applied to theirs. With the result that Professor Dowden, usually perceptive, was able to gloss ll. 9-10 as meaning, 'you need not count me when merely counting the *number* of those who hold you dear, but when estimating the *worth* of your possessions, you must have regard to me' ! While Knox Pooler was able to gloss 'store's account' as 'the inventory of your property' ! Both explanations are mere flummery, of course. 'Store's account' means simply the number of men the lady had accommodated. There are other plays on words throughout the sonnet, 'come', 'things of great receipt', 'hold', 'a something sweet' : drop the Victorian humbug and we may laugh as the Elizabethans laughed.

137

Thou blind fool, love, what dost thou to mine eyes
That they behold and see not what they see?
They know what beauty is, see where it lies,
Yet what the best is take the worst to be.
If eyes, corrupt by over-partial looks,
Be anchored in the bay where all men ride,
Why of eyes' falsehood hast thou forgèd hooks
Whereto the judgment of my heart is tied?
Why should my heart think that a several plot
Which my heart knows the wide world's common place?
Or mine eyes seeing this, say this is not,
To put fair truth upon so foul a face?
    In things right true my heart and eyes have erred,
    And to this false plague are they now transferred.

137

Love, you blind fool, what do you do to my eyes that they behold and see not what they see ? They know what beauty is and see where it lies, yet take what is the worst for the best. If my eyes, corrupted by the partiality of love, are anchored in the bay where all men ride, why have you forged hooks out of the eyes' falsehood to tie up the judgment of my heart ? Why should my heart think that an individual private plot which it knows is common to all the world ? Or my eyes, seeing this, assert that it is not so, so as to impute fair truth to so foul a face ? In matters of truth my heart and eyes have erred, and in consequence are now infected with falseness.

————

After those two sonnets, comic in their approach, we have a serious one, for Shakespeare is seriously involved, and becomes infatuated with the lady, though he has no illusions about her. Neither have we, any longer. Getting to know her better — he cannot help himself — he becomes more and more uncomplimentary. She is a loose woman, a 'bay where all men ride' (the image is from shipping ; 'ride' was the regular Elizabethan nautical term, but here it has a double meaning), 'the wide world's common place'. Such sonnets cannot have been for her eye ; they were for Southampton's. Perhaps they did him some good, and helped him to emancipate himself from her clutches. Perhaps they were intended to help, as well as amuse, him.

138

When my love swears that she is made of truth
I do believe her, though I know she lies,
That she might think me some untutored youth,
Unlearnèd in the world's false subtleties.
Thus vainly thinking that she thinks me young,
Although she knows my days are past the best,
Simply I credit her false-speaking tongue —
On both sides thus is simple truth suppressed.
But wherefore says she not she is unjust?
And wherefore say not I that I am old?
O, love's best habit is in seeming trust,
And age in love loves not to have years told.
　　Therefore I lie with her and she with me,
　　And in our faults by lies we flattered be.

138

When my love swears that she is true I believe her, although I know
she is lying, so that she may think me some inexperienced youth,
unacquainted with the world's falsities. Thus vainly thinking
that she thinks me young, although she knows quite well that I am
past my prime, pretending simply to credit her lying tongue — so
that on both sides the simple truth is suppressed. But why does she
not say that she is untrue ? And why don't I say that I am old ?
It is best in love to seem to trust, and age in love loves not to have
years counted. So I lie with her and she with me, and in our faults
we are soothed by lies.

This takes us further into Shakespeare's relationship with the lady : it is
purely sexual, utterly unromantic — unlike that with the young Earl.
Emilia has become his mistress : she was six years younger, closer to
Southampton in age. In this relationship, too, Shakespeare is much the
older : it redoubles his consciousness of his age. Hence the mutual
hypocrisies on the surface, for underneath there is Shakespeare's honest
candour. From the literary point of view there is the uncompromising
realism with which he describes it all : it has been said — rightly — that
there is no woman like Shakespeare's in all the sonnet-literature of the
Renaissance. Most of them are abstractions or wraiths ; this one is of
flesh and blood.

139

O call not me to justify the wrong
That thy unkindness lays upon my heart ;
Wound me not with thine eye, but with thy tongue ;
Use power with power, and slay me not by art.
Tell me thou lov'st elsewhere, but in my sight,
Dear heart, forbear to glance thine eye aside :
What need'st thou wound with cunning, when thy might
Is more than my o'er-pressed defence can bide ?
Let me excuse thee : ah, my love well knows
Her pretty looks have been mine enemies,
And therefore from my face she turns my foes,
That they elsewhere might dart their injuries :
 Yet do not so, but since I am near slain
 Kill me outright with looks and rid my pain.

139

Do not ask me to justify the wrong that your unkindness lays upon
my heart ; do not wound me with your eye, but with your tongue ;
use your power direct, not kill me by artifice. Tell me you love
elsewhere, but in my sight, dear heart, forbear to look at others :
why need you deliberately wound when your power over me is
more than my defences can stand ? Let me excuse you : my love
knows well that her pretty looks have undone me, and therefore
she turns her eyes away from me that they may inflict their injuries
elsewhere : do not do so, but — since I am at your mercy — kill
me straight with looks and put an end to my pain.

Sincere, in spite of the literary artifice, but humiliating — Shakespeare has
to accept the fact that she loves elsewhere, but begs that she should not
make it so clear in his presence. The phrasing of l. 3 reminds us of *3 Henry
VI*, V. vi. 26, 'kill me with thy weapon, not with words'. There is a
reflection in *Romeo and Juliet*, II, iv. 14, 'stabbed with a white wench's
black eye'.

140

Be wise as thou art cruel, do not press
My tongue-tied patience with too much disdain,
Lest sorrow lend me words and words express
The manner of my pity-wanting pain.
If I might teach thee wit, better it were
Though not to love, yet, love, to tell me so ;
As testy sick men when their deaths be near
No news but health from their physicians know.
For if I should despair I should go mad,
And in my madness might speak ill of thee ;
Now this ill-wresting world is grown so bad
Mad slanderers by mad ears believèd be.
    That I may not be so, nor thou belied,
      Bear thine eyes straight though thy proud heart go
      wide.

140

Be wise as you are cruel, and do not regard my silent patience with too much scorn, lest grief lends me words, and words express how much I suffer from your lack of pity. If I might instruct you — though you do not love, it were better to tell me that you do ; as peevish sick men on their death-beds hear nothing from their doctors but of recovery. For if I were to despair I should go mad, and in my madness might speak ill of you ; now this world, that wrests everything to the worst, is grown so bad that mad slanderers are believed by mad ears. That I may not be such, nor you slandered, keep your eyes straight ahead, though your proud heart goes astray.

Now that we know the kind of woman she was, l. 5 has a certain edge on it. To Elizabethans 'wit' meant intelligence ; 'if I might teach thee wit' — Shakespeare might certainly give her a point or two here. She could not but play him false.

141

In faith, I do not love thee with mine eyes
For they in thee a thousand errors note,
But 'tis my heart that loves what they despise
Who, in despite of view, is pleased to dote.
Nor are mine ears with thy tongue's tune delighted,
Nor tender feeling to base touches prone,
Nor taste, nor smell, desire to be invited
To any sensual feast with thee alone :
But my five wits, nor my five senses can
Dissuade one foolish heart from serving thee,
Who leaves unswayed the likeness of a man,
Thy proud heart's slave and vassal wretch to be :
    Only my plague thus far I count my gain
    That she that makes me sin awards me pain.

141

In truth, I do not love you with my eyes, for they note a thousand
defects in you : it is my heart that loves what they disapprove —
which, in spite of what it sees, continues to dote. Nor are my ears
delighted with the sound of your voice ; nor tender feeling, prone
to low tricks, nor taste, nor smell desire to be invited to any sensual
feast with you alone. Yet neither my five wits nor my five senses
can dissuade one foolish heart from serving you, leaving only the
likeness of a man to be your proud heart's slave and vassal. But
thus far I count my plague my gain, that she that makes me sin
awards me punishment.

———

More difficult than usual to render in modern English. L. 6, the Elizabethan word 'touch' means 'trick' ; we still have some sense of it in our
slang word, to touch a person, i.e. for money. The language of the Dark
Lady sequence is far from elevated — in contrast with that to Southampton. Nor has that been noted.

The reference to plague in l. 13, and that in Sonnet 137, l. 14, remind
us that we are not far from the plague year 1593.

142

Love is my sin, and thy dear virtue hate,
Hate of my sin, grounded on sinful loving.
O, but with mine compare thou thine own state
And thou shalt find it merits not reproving ;
Or, if it do, not from those lips of thine
That have profaned their scarlet ornaments
And sealed false bonds of love as oft as mine,
Robbed others' beds' revenues of their rents.
Be it lawful I love thee, as thou lov'st those
Whom thine eyes woo as mine importune thee :
Root pity in thy heart that, when it grows,
Thy pity may deserve to pitied be.
    If thou dost seek to have what thou dost hide,
    By self-example mayst thou be denied.

142

Love is my sin, and your best virtue dislike — dislike of my sin, grounded as it is in sinful loving. But compare your own state with mine, and you will find it does not deserve reproof ; or, if it does, not from your lips that have profaned themselves and sealed false bonds of love as often as mine, while you have robbed others' beds of their dues. Let me then love you, as you love those whom your eyes woo — as mine importune you : take pity in your heart so that later it may win you pity in return. If you seek to have what you yourself withhold, you may be denied in keeping with your own example.

———

The Dark Lady sonnets are more difficult to render in modern English than the Southampton sequence, the thought is more tortured, the language more powerful — and less beautiful. The psychological situation, always obviously a real one, is all the more convincing now we can recognise the familiar humiliations of an older person in love with a younger. It was not for this young woman to object to Shakespeare's infatuation on the ground of its being adulterous, considering what she was. Such is the argument : the time would come when she would need pity. In a few years it did, as we know now.

Impossible to put more psychological complexity and human experience more concisely than in ll. 9-10 :

> Be it lawful I love thee, as thou lov'st those
> Whom thine eyes woo as mine importune thee.

They sum up the insatiable human pursuit of one another.

143

Lo, as a careful housewife runs to catch
One of her feathered creatures broke away,
Sets down her babe and makes all swift dispatch
In pursuit of the thing she would have stay ;
Whilst her neglected child holds her in chase,
Cries to catch her whose busy care is bent
To follow that which flies before her face,
Not prizing her poor infant's discontent :
So runn'st thou after that which flies from thee,
Whilst I thy babe chase thee afar behind ;
But if thou catch thy hope, turn back to me
And play the mother's part, kiss me, be kind.

    So will I pray that thou mayst have thy will,
    If thou turn back and my loud crying still.

143

Just as a careful housewife, running after one of her chickens getting away, sets down her child and hurries after the thing she wants to stop escaping ; whilst her child, neglected, follows after, crying to catch her who is bent on following that which flies from her, not caring for her poor infant's feelings : so you run after that which flies from you, whilst I, your child, chase after you far behind. But if you get what you want, turn back to me and play the mother's part, kiss me and be kind. Then I will pray that you may have your will, if you will turn back and console me.

———

In this equivocal situation, with its growing torment and anxiety, it is nice to think that Shakespeare's humour did not desert him : he could see the funny side in himself chasing after the young woman, while she was chasing someone else. He was ready to accept that she should have her 'will' — here is that word again — provided that he might share in her favours. The sage Victorian, Sir Sidney Lee, thought 'the moral somewhat equivocal . . . There is some suggestion of a *ménage à trois*.' I fear there was more than that.

This simple country scene may be said to take place 'behind the barn', in the old American phrase.

144

Two loves I have, of comfort and despair,
Which like two spirits do suggest me still :
The better angel is a man right fair,
The worser spirit a woman coloured ill.
To win me soon to hell, my female evil
Tempteth my better angel from my side,
And would corrupt my saint to be a devil,
Wooing his purity with her foul pride.
And whether that my angel be turned fiend
Suspect I may, yet not directly tell ;
But being both from me, both to each friend,
I guess one angel in another's hell.
    Yet this shall I ne'er know, but live in doubt,
    Till my bad angel fire my good one out.

Two loves possess me, the one comforting, the other despairing, which like two spirits tempt me on : the better angel is a man and fair, the worser spirit is a woman dark in favour. To involve me more — my female evil tempts my better angel away from me, and would seduce his purity with her ill pride. And whether my angel be corrupted, though I suspect, I cannot tell directly ; but both being away from me, and each agreeing with the other, I guess that one angel is in the other's hell. Yet this I shall never know, but live in suspicion, till my bad angel fires my good one out.

This presents in serious terms the situation rendered humorously in the previous sonnet — in itself enough to show how all these sonnets hang together, and belong to the same period. After the 'will' sonnets we now have variations on the theme of 'hell', turned ingeniously to a conceit with appropriate imagery, 'spirits', 'angels', 'devils', 'fiends'. How clever — and naughty — it all is ! This particular group coheres with Sonnets 40-42 in the Southampton sequence, and deals with the same experience from another angle. In those Shakespeare dealt with it from the point of view of his friendship with Southampton, much more movingly :

> That thou hast her, it is not all my grief,
> And yet it may be said I loved her dearly ;
> That she hath thee, is of my wailing chief,
> A loss in love that touches me more nearly.

In l. 12,

> I guess one angel in another's hell.

Knox Pooler has the absurdity to guess an allusion to the game of barley-break. Hyder Rollins is nearer the mark in seeing in l. 14 the implication in 'fire out' of venereal disease, rampant in Elizabethan society.

145

Those lips that Love's own hand did make
Breathed forth the sound that said 'I hate'
To me that languished for her sake.
But when she saw my woeful state,
Straight in her heart did mercy come,
Chiding that tongue that ever sweet
Was used in giving gentle doom :
And taught it thus anew to greet,
'I hate' she altered with an end,
That followed it as gentle day
Doth follow night who, like a fiend,
From heaven to hell is flown away.
   'I hate' from hate away she threw,
   And saved my life, saying 'not you'.

145

Those lips that Love's own hand made breathed the words 'I hate'
to me that languished for her. But when she saw my sad condition,
mercy came into her heart, chiding the tongue that was accustomed
to be sweet in pronouncing one's doom ; and taught it a new
greeting. She altered 'I hate' with an end that followed it as gently
as day does night, which, like a fiend, is flown from heaven to hell.
'I hate' she threw away from hate and saved my life, adding 'not
you'.

———

Some have rejected this sonnet as not Shakespeare's, simply because it is
different and in tetrameters. Hyder Rollins is more sensible : 'I see no
especial reason for rejecting 145. The poet need not always have been
harping on his real or his imaginary mistress's blackness and falsity, but
may sometimes have cajoled her with praises of her kindness. He has
pleaded for his lady's pity in 132, 133, 140 and 142, and here she grants it.
Women, if fiction may be believed, not infrequently do so, even when
they are false.'

   Even this is not particularly percipient ; for observe the imagery of
'fiend' and 'heaven and hell' continued from the previous sonnet, that
shows us that this one is quite right where it is. We have observed the
tact and rhythm by which Shakespeare varies his serious pieces by something in lighter vein. Even with this light, yet unmistakably Shake-
spearean piece — cf. ll. 6-7 — there is a comparison with *Lucrece*, ll. 1534
foll.

> 'It cannot be', quoth she, 'that so much guile' —
> She would have said — 'can lurk in such a look' ;
> But Tarquin's shape came in her mind the while,
> And from her tongue 'can lurk' from 'cannot' took.

146

Poor soul, the centre of my sinful earth,
. . . these rebel powers that thee array,
Why dost thou pine within and suffer dearth,
Painting thy outward walls so costly gay ?
Why so large cost, having so short a lease,
Dost thou upon thy fading mansion spend ?
Shall worms, inheritors of this excess,
Eat up thy charge ? is this thy body's end ?
Then, soul, live thou upon thy servant's loss,
And let that pine to aggravate thy store ;
Buy terms divine in selling hours of dross,
Within be fed, without be rich no more :
    So shalt thou feed on death, that feeds on men,
    And death once dead, there's no more dying then.

———

Another variation, this has been much admired by philosophically-minded critics ; we may instance Santayana : 'this sonnet contains more than a natural religious emotion inspired by a single event. It contains reflection. . . . A mind that habitually ran into such thoughts would be philosophically pious ; it would be spiritual. . . . The Sonnets are spiritual, but, with the doubtful exception of 146, they are not Christian.'

I wonder whether this lofty sentiment does not contain a little philosophical humbug of its own ? I do not feel that the Sonnets are spiritual : they are altogether this-worldly and human, sensual and psychologically subtle — very Renaissance in fact.

It is interesting to find the word 'earth', used for body in l. 1, appearing in this sense in the neighbouring *Love's Labour's Lost*, IV. iii. 69, 'fair sun, which on my earth doth shine', and *Romeo and Juliet*, II. i. 2.

146

Poor soul, the centre of my sinful bearing these rebel powers that envelop you, why do you pine within and suffer want, while painting your outer walls so gaily ? Why, having so short a lease, do you spend so largely upon your fading mansion ? Shall worms, inheritors of this extravagance, eat up what you have spent so much on ? Is this the body's end ? Then, soul, live upon what the body loses, and leave that in want to increase your strength ; purchase eternity by selling worthless hours ; be fed within, care no more for outward glory : so will you feed on Death, as Death feeds on men, and Death once dead, there is no more dying.

———

Can I go forward when my heart is here ?
Turn back, dull earth, and find thy centre out.

In l. 2 it is vexing that the compositor mistakenly repeated 'my sinful earth' at the beginning of the line, from the end of the previous one. The sense demands some such word as 'feeding'. In the same line there has been a lot of discussion about the word 'array'. I do not see why : best to take it in its simple, straightforward sense. The last line is famous and much quoted : the sentiment, of course, Pauline.

Perhaps we may compare this with an earlier attempt, Sonnet 114, to catch up with, or express himself in, the new metaphysical fashion.

147

My love is as a fever, longing still
For that which longer nurseth the disease ;
Feeding on that which doth preserve the ill,
The uncertain sickly appetite to please.
My reason, the physician to my love,
Angry that his prescriptions are not kept,
Hath left me, and I desperate now approve
Desire is death, which physic did except.
Past cure I am, now reason is past care,
And frantic-mad with evermore unrest ;
My thoughts and my discourse as madmen's are,
At random from the truth vainly expressed.
   For I have sworn thee fair, and thought thee bright,
   Who art as black as hell, as dark as night.

147

My love is like a fever, still longing for that which increases the disease, feeding on that which prolongs the illness, to please the sick appetite. My reason, my physician, angry that his prescriptions are not kept, has left me, and desperate I find that desire, which took exception to physic, is death. Now reason is past caring, I am past cure, and frantic with continual unrest ; my thoughts and discourse are like a madman's, at random from the truth. For I have sworn you fair and thought of you as bright, who are dark as night and black as hell.

―――――

With this poem we are back with the theme of 'hell' and Shakespeare's familiar vein, concerned not with his soul and death, but with the facts of life. And also there is his double-mindedness. The sonnet may have a literary point of departure from a poem in Sidney's *Arcadia*, ending,

> Sick to the death, still loving my disease ;

at the same time, it is an expression of personal experience. Shakespeare uses his experience as matter for literature so self-awarely that the result sometimes reads like a literary exercise. However, in spite of the exaggeration, one cannot doubt the sincerity of ll. 7-8. On the other hand, so far from l. 12 —

> At random from the truth vainly expressed —

being the case, he expresses his frantic condition with complete control. This is as poets should be, but it is sometimes difficult to know precisely where one has Shakespeare. I hope this may contribute to explaining a characteristic of him as a writer as to which all agree.

148

O me ! what eyes hath love put in my head,
Which have no correspondence with true sight ;
Or, if they have, where is my judgment fled
That censures falsely what they see aright ?
If that be fair whereon my false eyes dote,
What means the world to say it is not so ?
If it be not, then love doth well denote
Love's eye is not so true as all men's : no,
How can it ? O, how can love's eye be true,
That is so vexed with watching and with tears ?
No marvel then, though I mistake my view ;
The sun itself sees not till heaven clears.
   O cunning love, with tears thou keep'st me blind,
   Lest eyes well-seeing thy foul faults should find.

148

What eyes has love put in my head, which do not correspond with
true sight ; or, if they do, where is my judgment that judges falsely
what they see correctly ? If what my false eyes dote on is fair, what
does the world mean to say that it is not ? If it is not, then it shows
that love's eye is not so true as all men's. No : how can it be ?
How can love's eye be true that is so vexed with watching and
weeping ? It is no wonder, then, that I am mistaken in my sight ;
the sun itself does not see till heaven clears. O cunning love : you
keep me blind with tears, lest clear-seeing eyes should notice your
foul faults.

Here is Shakespeare repeating himself, yet to give the theme a different
twist. L. 6 tells us that other people knew quite well what Emilia was ;
so did Shakespeare, but he was blinded by love, or — we should say — sex.
One cannot doubt the sincerity of l. 10. In l. 3 note the characteristic
apposition, 'Or, if they have', which occurs before in the Sonnets. In
l. 8 observe the audacity of the ending with a colon and a 'no'. There
has been much dispute about this punctuation, Sir Sidney Lee expressing
the view that 'no particular sanctity attaches to this perplexing punctuation'. The punctuation, in fact, is most effective and clear, and necessary
to the sense. In l. 13 the gentlemanly Dowden (he was an Irishman) opines
that 'here Shakespeare is perhaps speaking of his mistress, but if so, he
views her as Love personified'!

149

Canst thou, O cruel, say I love thee not,
When I against myself with thee partake?
Do I not think on thee when I forgot
Am of myself, all tyrant, for thy sake?
Who hateth thee that I do call my friend;
On whom frown'st thou that I do fawn upon?
Nay, if thou lour'st on me, do I not spend
Revenge upon myself with present moan?
What merit do I in myself respect
That is so proud thy service to despise,
When all my best doth worship thy defect,
Commanded by the motion of thine eyes?
    But, love, hate on, for now I know thy mind;
    Those that can see thou lov'st, and I am blind.

149

Cruel one, can you say that I do not love you, when I take sides with you against myself? Am I not thinking of you when I forget myself for your sake, tyrant as you are? Who that dislikes you do I call friend; and whom do I fawn upon that you disapprove? No: if you frown on me, do I not react immediately with pain and grief? What quality do I respect in myself that is too proud to serve you, when all the best in me worships your very defects, in subjection as I am to your eyes? But love, hate me as you will, for now I know your mind; you love those that can see you as you are, and I am blind.

This group of sonnets clearly belongs together; the theme is Shakespeare's infatuation, though without illusions. The theme is the conflict between what his mind tells him and his infatuation. It is pretty clear that the young woman did not want the poet, that she had other lovers, and that for a time she had got hold of Southampton. Evidently the older man did not appeal to her: he had to put up with what he could get. This sonnet reverses the hitherto frequent refrain, with the woman complaining this time that Shakespeare does not care for her. Not caring for him, alas, does not prevent this kind of reproach. She has enemies, who speak ill of her; Shakespeare takes her side, though he knows better. How convincing it all is! — like a modern novel, unlike anything else in Elizabethan sonnet-literature.

L. 5 reflects Psalm 139: 'Do not I hate them, O Lord, that hate thee: and am not I grieved with those that rise up against thee?'

150

O, from what power hast thou this powerful might
With insufficiency my heart to sway ?
To make me give the lie to my true sight,
And swear that brightness doth not grace the day ?
Whence hast thou this becoming of things ill,
That in the very refuse of thy deeds
There is such strength and warrantise of skill
That, in my mind, thy worst all best exceeds ?
Who taught thee how to make me love thee more,
The more I hear and see just cause of hate ?
O, though I love what others do abhor,
With others thou shouldst not abhor my state.
    If thy unworthiness raised love in me,
    More worthy I to be beloved of thee.

150

From what do you derive this extraordinary power to sway my heart with your very defects ? To make me give the lie to what I see quite clearly, and swear that black is white ? Whence this ability to make bad things seem good, so that in the very refuse of your deeds there is such assurance that, in my mind, your worst is better than other people's best ? Who taught you how to make me love you more, the more I hear and see good reason to detest ? Yet, though I love what others abhor, you should not join with others in abhorring my condition and circumstances. If your unworthiness made me love you, I am all the more worthy of your love.

Now that there is no mystery about the mistress, we see how truthful and convincing a portrait of her this was. But l. 13 reveals something new : it was her 'unworthiness', her pitiable situation that aroused Shakespeare's love. And now we know what that was, v. Introduction, p. xxxiv.

L. 4 is paralleled not long after in *Romeo and Juliet*, III. v. 18 :

> I am content, so thou wilt have it so.
> I'll say yon grey is not the morning's eye.

151

Love is too young to know what conscience is,
Yet who knows not conscience is born of love ?
Then, gentle cheater, urge not my amiss,
Lest guilty of my faults thy sweet self prove.
For, thou betraying me, I do betray
My nobler part to my gross body's treason :
My soul doth tell my body that he may
Triumph in love : flesh stays no farther reason,
But rising at thy name doth point out thee
As his triumphant prize. Proud of this pride,
He is contented thy poor drudge to be,
To stand in thy affairs, fall by thy side.
   No want of conscience hold it that I call
   Her 'love', for whose dear love I rise and fall.

After the previous serious sonnets, we have, for relaxation, this humorous, naughty one. A Victorian scholar found it 'impossible to admit that Shakespeare would, in his own person, address to *any* woman such gross *double-entendres* as are contained in ll. 8-14'. Hyder Rollins comments, with greater respect for truth, 'to which one might reply that the woman in question is represented as a prostitute, who presumably enjoyed grossness'. But we must not conclude that the lady was precisely a prostitute because she was of easy virtue. The Edwardian Liberal, J. M. Robertson, described it as 'a highly anomalous sonnet, isolated in tone and purport from all the others, and introducing a grossness nowhere else to be found in the Quarto'. To which Hyder Rollins very properly replies : 'But 20, 138, and 144 are equally gross', and adds, 'the majority of editors and critics pass this sonnet by in silence, and probably most readers fail to understand it.'

151

Love is too young to know what conscience is, yet who does not know that conscience is born of love ? Then, sweet cheat, do not upbraid me with my faults, lest it is you who prove guilty of them. For, if you betray me, I betray my nobler part to the flesh ; my soul tells my flesh to triumph in love, and it awaits no further encouragement, but, rising at your name, points to you as the target. Swelling with this encouragement, he is contented to serve you, to stand by you and fall by your side. Do not hold it for want of conscience that I call her 'love', for whose love I rise and fall.

———

I do not propose to explain what most readers should, without humbug, understand. The naughty phraseology of the sestet is paralleled not long after in *Romeo and Juliet*, II. i. 23 foll. :

> Mercutio :   'twould anger him
> To raise a spirit in his mistress' circle
> Of some strange nature, letting it there stand
> Till she had laid it and conjured it down.

Professor Tucker, who opines that 'this composition is one which, from the nature of its contents, might well be let die', nevertheless enlightens us usefully with the information, to help us with l. 10, that 'flesh is "proud" when it swells'.

152

In loving thee thou know'st I am forsworn,
But thou art twice forsworn, to me love swearing :
In act thy bed-vow broke and new faith torn,
In vowing new hate after new love bearing.
But why of two oaths' breach do I accuse thee,
When I break twenty ? I am perjured most,
For all my vows are oaths but to misuse thee,
And all my honest faith in thee is lost.
For I have sworn deep oaths of thy deep kindness,
Oaths of thy love, thy truth, thy constancy,
And, to enlighten thee, gave eyes to blindness,
Or made them swear against the thing they see.
   For I have sworn thee fair : more perjured I,
   To swear against the truth so foul a lie.

152

You know that in loving you I am forsworn, but you are twice forsworn in swearing love to me, in breaking your promise in bed and making a new breach after a reconciliation. But why do I accuse you of breaking two oaths, when I break twenty ? I am more perjured than you, for all my vows are oaths to abuse, and all my faith in you is gone. For I have sworn to your kindness and love, your truth and constancy ; and, to lend you light, blinded my eyes or made them swear against what they see. For I have sworn you fair, and am all the more perjured to swear so foul a lie against the truth.

———

This bodes the end of the relationship, when Shakespeare says,

> And all my honest faith in thee is lost.

It has been a singularly unhappy one, giving little satisfaction to either partner. We learn from this that there had been a reconciliation, followed by a new breach. L. 3 has usually been taken to indicate that the lady was married ; this we now know to have been true, but the context here refers to a vow she had given Shakespeare when in bed with him, after a breach. Hence the 'two oaths' breach' with which he charges her. Evidently she did not much care for him, and perhaps this was the end of the relationship, a suitable juncture at which to terminate it. We learn that Forman's experience three years later was no more satisfactory, and his impression of her character even more unfavourable. But he was not a victim of infatuation or under her spell.

We see, then, that these sonnets belong together as a group, carrying on the themes of feverish love, of the conflict between what Shakespeare well knows and what he wants, of lying to himself against the evidence, of faith forsworn. What a story, described with candour, expressing everything, physical as well as mental ! Now the woman wants to end it. Full of anguish as it has been, the experience has at least provided a subject. Art redeems life.

153

Cupid laid by his brand and fell asleep :
A maid of Dian's this advantage found,
And his love-kindling fire did quickly steep
In a cold valley-fountain of that ground :
Which borrowed from this holy fire of love
A dateless lively heat, still to endure,
And grew a seething bath, which yet men prove
Against strange maladies a sovereign cure.
But at my mistress' eye love's brand new-fired,
The boy for trial needs would touch my breast :
I, sick withal, the help of bath desired
And thither hied, a sad distempered guest.
   But found no cure : the bath for my help lies
   Where Cupid got new fire, my mistress' eyes.

153

Cupid laid his brand by and fell asleep : one of Diana's maidens took advantage of this and quickly steeped his love-kindling fire in a cold fountain in the valley : which borrowed from this sacred fire a continual heat, to go on for ever, and become a seething bath, which men try as a cure against strange maladies. But Cupid must needs touch my breast with love's brand, new-fired at my mistress' eyes : I, sick with it, desired the help of the bath and went there, a sadly distempered patient. But I found no cure : the bath to aid me is where Cupid got new fire, my mistress' eyes.

———

This and the following sonnet are two versions of the same theme, and they are not unsuitably placed as a kind of coda to the Dark Lady Sonnets, to which they relate. They serve quite well to round off the affair, which comes to a sudden end — with Emilia breaking off on her side, Shakespeare to the bath — this was the usual Elizabethan phrase for going to Bath — to cure his distemper.

J. W. Mackail was 'inclined to think' that these sonnets 'are not by Shakespeare at all'. There is no reason whatever to doubt that they are his : they bear every mark of his characteristic ingenuity and suggestiveness.

154

The little Love-god lying once asleep
Laid by his side his heart-inflaming brand,
Whilst many nymphs that vowed chaste life to keep
Came tripping by ; but in her maiden hand
The fairest votary took up that fire
Which many legions of true hearts had warmed ;
And so the general of hot desire
Was sleeping by a virgin hand disarmed.
This branch she quenchèd in a cool well by,
Which from love's fire took heat perpetual,
Growing a bath and helpful remedy
For men diseased ; but I, my mistress' thrall,
    Came there for cure, and this by that I prove,
    Love's fire heats water, water cools not love.

154

The little god of love, lying once asleep, laid his heart-inflaming brand by his side, whilst many nymphs vowed to chastity came tripping by. The fairest of them took in her hand the fire that had warmed legions of hearts ; and so the generator of hot desire was disarmed, sleeping, by a virgin. She quenched this brand in a cool well near by, which took perpetual heat from love's fire, becoming a medicinal bath for men diseased. But I, my mistress' slave, came there for cure, and by that I prove this : love's fire heats water, water does not cool love.

For what Shakespeare had in mind, ll. 1 and 7, it is interesting to compare *Love's Labour's Lost* of just this time, III. i. 170 foll. :

> This senior-junior, giant-dwarf, Dan Cupid . . .
> Dread prince of plackets, king of codpieces,
> Sole imperator, and great general
> Of trotting paritors.

So much for Mackail.

73 74 75 76 77 10 9 8 7 6 5 4 3 2 1